Mandalas
for Meditation

Mandalas
for Meditation

Ruediger Dahlke

Sterling Publishing Co., Inc.
New York

For Naomi-Magdalena

Library of Congress Cataloging-in-Publication Data Available

10 9 8 7 6 5 4 3 2 1

Published in 2001 by Sterling Publishing Co., Inc.
387 Park Avenue South, New York, NY 10016
Originally published in Germany under the title *Arbeitsbuch
zur Mandala-Therapie: Mit 166 Mandalas zum Ausmalen* by Heinrich Hugendubel Verlag
Holzstrasse 28, 80469 Munich, Germany
©1999 by Heinrich Hugendubel Verlag
English Translation © 2001 by Sterling Publishing
Distributed in Canada by Sterling Publishing
℅ Canadian Manda Group, One Atlantic Avenue, Suite 105
Toronto, Ontario, M6K 3E7, Canada
Distributed in Great Britain and Europe by Cassell PLC
Wellington House, 125 Strand, London WC2R 0BB, England
Distributed in Australia by Capricorn Link (Australia) Pty. Ltd.
P.O. Box 704, Windsor, NSW 2756 Australia

Sterling ISBN 0-8069-2519-1

Table of contents

Acknowledgments

I would like to thank Elisabeth Mitteregger, Julia and
Andrea Druckenthaner, and Willi Weis for their support in
creating the mandalas,
my wife Margit for her support and ideas, and
Helen Heisserer for her editorial work.

*"I realized more and more clearly
that the mandala is the center;
it is the expression of all life;
it is the path of individuation."*
C.G. JUNG

Preface

*I*nspired by C.G. Jung's work and encouraged by personal interest, I introduced coloring mandalas into psychotherapy 20 years ago. I was not sure whether something so "childish" would succeed. In the early 1980s, I started writing the book *Mandalas of the World*, partly for my own enjoyment and partly to have a coloring book to give my patients to accompany their therapies. I could not have anticipated that coloring mandalas would become so popular.

In a motor home, I drove from cathedral to cathedral and copied the Gothic window roses, which began to fascinate me more and more and which to this day I regard as the pinnacle of mandala culture. The cathedrals slowly revealed to me secrets that seemed to originate with the mandalas; some even went further back than the mandalas themselves. Soon I started to discover mandalas everywhere, seemingly accidentally, in nature and in culture. I saw more and more clearly that everything is connected to mandalas. Since then, mandalas have accompanied me with every step I take, and their secret—of the center— has an unending fascination for me.

Even though I was working with great commitment and enthusiasm, I was unable to find a publisher for a long time. My mandalas and I received one friendly rejection letter after another. Now, twenty years later, there is hardly a publisher who has not jumped on the mandala bandwagon. The coloring book concept of *Mandalas of the World* has been copied numerous times, each one with a slightly different emphasis. The wonderful thing about this is the apparently great and still increasing demand for mandalas. There is a place for mandalas once again in our society, where they seemed to have been lost for such a long time. They have done it on their own without advertisements or press releases. They were passed from one mandala lover to the next in a massive wave that is still growing.

As I mentioned earlier, I had a hard time in the early eighties finding a publisher for my mandalas and getting people excited about them. This was largely because nobody was convinced that something so simple could really work. But mandalas caught on—big time. As the "father" of the mandala coloring "epidemic" and with over 20 years' experience in dealing with mandalas, I would now like to do my bit to ensure that they remain popular.

This is why I feel it is time to go (or color) one step further and make my therapeutic experiences available to a larger audience. It again takes the shape of the now traditional— anything but revolutionary—personal mandala coloring book, *Mandalas for Meditation*.

As far as the mandalas in the second part of this book are concerned, we have again relied on tried and tested manual work. We made a conscious decision to forego the kind of graphic perfection that is possible nowadays with computers since mandalas can only be considered perfect in their immaterial centers.

In fact, outside—on the periphery that symbolizes the polar world of contradictions—perfection would be inappropriate. This, at least, is how people see it who either come from mandala cultures or who appreciate them. Regardless, since the computer has become an integral part of our society, Willi Weis used one to create his ancient principle mandalas as well as the mandalas in the chapter "Modern Day Mandalas." With these exceptions, we have chosen to use only the tools that would have been available to the builders of Gothic cathedrals with their stained glass (mandala) windows—a compass, a protractor, and a ruler.

Why a Coloring Book for Adults?

I am frequently asked this question, sometimes even quite aggressively—coloring, after all, is for children. Generally speaking, coloring mandalas can be recommended for any age. Since they encompass life in its entirety, they accompany all the stages of life. It is certainly no coincidence that coloring books are given to children to practice understanding and following established structures. Coloring a mandala's predetermined framework is a useful exercise to practice adapting to a framework that is already in existence and which cannot fundamentally change. When we color a mandala, we are doing just this. We can, and should, give it our own "inimitable" or "individual" touch. If a thousand people were to color the same mandala, no two would be the same, despite the fact that all mandalas have the same structure. Therefore, every time children color in a book, they enliven it with their own special colors and also learn to follow certain rules. Many of the mandala books today play down this aspect and emphasize boundless freedom instead. This of course, keeps with our time, but not with life and consequently, not with mandalas. That aside, most children—big or small—enjoy coloring mandalas; otherwise, there would not be such a demand for mandala books.

It is much more beneficial for most of us to color a mandala than to create one from scratch. The fact that creating one seems more enjoyable only indicates that there is a much greater inclination in our society towards the Sun principle, which deals with creativity, than towards the Saturn principle, which deals with following rules. Since each principle is irreplaceable, however, we struggle much more with Saturn-related problems, which we would generally prefer to ignore. When I look back over my two decades of medical and psychotherapeutic practice, I can relate many stories that deal with not observing (cosmic) laws—Saturn—but I have encountered far fewer problems that have their roots in unexpressed creativity. Quite a few people suffer from a combination of both problems, and people adhere too strictly to the laws of the world while ignoring the cosmic laws, making them unable to find the way back to their own lives due to a lack of initiative and creativity.

Therefore, it does make sense to practice creativity by painting or drawing freely and by gaining experience in overcoming barriers erected by society. It seems to me that it is much more important that we relearn to subordinate ourselves to the cosmic principles that rule our lives, whether we want them to or not. Coloring mandalas enables us to do this, which is why I think they are so incredibly successful.

When I talk about cosmic laws I am not just referring to the greater contexts, such as the laws of polarity or resonance, but also to ideas like a proper diet and achieving a natural relationship between rest and activity. As humans, we were born omnivores with strong vegetarian tendencies. So we should not be surprised when, as we age, we develop conditions such as arteriosclerosis, rheumatism, etc., due to an exaggerated daily intake of protein. We are not abiding by the laws and have to pay for it. The fact that the majority of people ignores these laws does not change their validity. The realization and acceptance of these basic principles is the most effective step towards getting one's life in order, as I have witnessed for many years in my seminars.

Western society, which is pretty much in love with the idea of being able to decide and to control everything all the time and disregards all laws and boundaries, has ignored mandalas for a long time. This is probably due to the fact that mandalas make us realize that there are limitations in life, which means that our lives are predestined.

The last two decades have brought to our attention that our society of "doers" has limits. We have reached these limits and have realized that our society has become dangerous to us and to our planet. This realization enabled mandalas to find their way back into our consciousness. People in industrialized nations are beginning to see that they do not have the means, let alone the power, to live their lives against the laws of creation. In fact, we do not even have control over the most significant stages of our lives or the passage from one to the next. Death is a good example. We make every effort to keep it at bay, but we have to realize that death is infinitely more powerful. Even though we are able remove organs in order ultimately to save the life of another person, these are only half-measures compared to the superior power and quiet dignity of death, which will always have the last word.

Just as with death, we really have no power to control change in our lives, but we will try just about anything so we can at least pretend we have some control. Puberty is a good example. After all, it is not pleasant when all of a sudden childhood games are not fun anymore and the wonderful years of childhood just seem to disappear. The young person does not feel at home anywhere, least of all in his or her own body. It would be a medical possibility to give girls, for example, anti-estrogens that are used in breast cancer treatment as a way to prevent puberty and control this stage of life. Thankfully, we have not taken things quite this far, but there are other stages of life where we have.

To sum everything up, we have to realize that our whole lives are a combination of filling in color and drawing freehand. Coloring books allow us to practice following set patterns. Coloring is more fundamental and occurs much earlier in life than drawing. The fact that so many adults resent it is due to the attitudes of our modern society and the consequent negation of reality. Although coloring is for children many adults enjoy it and many more can benefit from it.

Many times, things that are important for development are those that do not come easily. Therefore, it is good to learn first to accept what cannot be changed, before starting to shape that which corresponds to our decisions and our creative abilities. This realization is quite wonderfully expressed in the following prayer:

God grant me the serenity to accept the things I cannot change, the courage to change the things that I can, and the wisdom to know the difference.

Only when we have mastered the art of following set patterns and accepted that "Thy will be done," can we fulfill our creative potentials. Working with coloring books is equally important for children and for adults. When small and big children practice adhering to pre-determined structures, they symbolically learn to show humility towards creation, which will later enable them to express their creativity more freely and committedly. We can easily see that those people who show humility towards creation and who accept the greater framework of their lives are also the ones who enjoy great creative achievements.

Mandalas: Therapeutic Experiences

Introduction

A couple of years after *Mandalas of the World* was published, I received a letter from a young female doctor with a surprising story regarding the mandalas. On her way to becoming a specialist in neurology, she had to work a year's residency in a psychiatric ward. She was assigned to a geriatric ward where little therapeutic work was being done on the patients with psychiatric idiosyncrasies. Initially, the young doctor tried to work against this predominant attitude and introduce some therapeutic techniques. Over time, she tired of fighting the stubborn resistance of the psychiatrists and patients. By accident she came across the coloring pad that accompanied my book. As all else had already failed, she thought she would at least hand out some mandalas and coloring pencils, and the patients who felt like it could color them. Soon the entire ward was decorated with mandalas, and more and more people started to color them. It even seemed to be fun for the patients of whom nobody had expected this. Because it was so easy, no supervision was needed. Suddenly the doctor noticed the most amazing changes in her patients. Not only did they seem calmer and more centered, the overall atmosphere had become more harmonious and lighthearted. Two older ladies, who had not spoken for years and barely communicated otherwise, surprised everybody by starting to color the mandalas as well. When one of them started to talk again, the doctor could not help but feel that it had something to do with the mandalas. And when the second lady also began to communicate verbally, the young doctor became convinced that there must be some inherent secret in the mandalas. Sadly, when the young doctor left the psychiatric ward, the mandala wave came to an abrupt end.

I have since learned of many such experiences and stories that border on the miraculous. Unfortunately, they have never—as far as I am aware—been scientifically investigated, simply because scientists today just do not bother about phenomena like these. Which university or research group would fund a study on the effects of mandalas on psychiatric patients? The fact alone that there is no profit to be made from this may explain why we probably cannot expect any such studies in the future.

We have no choice but to draw conclusions from individual observations and experiences. I have many of these which are so touching that mere words are not enough to describe them. If we were to collate them in factual reports, we would lose an essential part of what makes mandalas so wonderful: their ability to emotionalize, center, and integrate people. We have very little experience, so far, with giving words to the process of human individuation, possibly because this society did not deem it worthy of attention until C.G. Jung came along. Only marginal groups on the fringes of society seem to care about it. This is surprising especially when we consider that most archaic cultures knew no other than this path of individuation. It seems that mandalas initiate this path of development, and since it is something very individual and particular to each person, the effects of mandalas are extremely varied and difficult to categorize. We could make a general statement and say that mandalas help with "becoming human." Now, this may sound a little strange to us in the western world since we consider ourselves human from the day we are born. Although this is definitely true from a legal point of view, it becomes quite problematic from a developmental-psychological point of view. In India it is generally believed that we have to struggle throughout our lives to become truly human. In western esoteric teachings, Gurdjieff assumed that a long and involved developmental process was necessary before a person could awaken to being truly human. So, it appears that mandalas help everybody at their respective stages of development.

As mentioned before, I once asked a group of several hundred people to color the same mandala, and no two of the finished mandalas were exactly alike. I did, however, have an interesting experience with one of our fasting groups with whom I played a popular mandala game, one that I would like to recommend here as a beginning exercise. I had the group split up into pairs and made each pair cut a mandala diagonally in two. I handed out coloring pencils and had them take their halves to opposite ends of the room. The object was to try and "tune in" to the other person so that both mandala halves would be colored as similarly as possible. When the mandala halves were put together after half an hour, we discovered—as always—some surprising coincidences, but no identical mandalas. We did, however, have an astonishing experience at the end of the week. Among the members of the group was an older married couple, and both had chosen different partners for this exercise. Their mandala halves were only a little bit similar to those of their chosen partners, but when we took the mandalas apart again on the last day so that everybody could take his or her half home, we "accidentally" made an amazing discovery. The halves that the spouses had colored were an almost perfect match. The statistical probability of this is about the same as winning the lottery. Both spouses were so touched that they shed tears, which is something that happens regularly when working with mandalas; they seem to connect to our deepest emotions. It was quite obvious that both had found their "better half" in the other. But the experience also showed something else: the couple was so tuned into one another that they were pretty much unable to tune into someone else.

Mandala games and exercises like these can lead us deeply into our emotional realms. The exercise above happens to be a very good test of intuitive abilities. While most do not experience anything more than accidental matches, there are always some who achieve similarities that go against all statistical probabilities.

Mandalas Reveal Who Belongs to Whom

The powerful symbolism of mandalas manifested itself dramatically in another exercise, although this time the result was not entirely positive for everybody involved. Everyone in the group had colored mandalas, which we then assembled into one big mandala and placed on the wall. A former partner of one of the members of the group happened to come in; we asked her which of the mandalas appealed to her most. Without hesitation she pointed to the mandala that her ex-husband had colored. He was just as surprised as she was, but it was his new girlfriend, who was also present, who had the strongest reaction and who was very concerned. A powerful group dynamic immediately developed between the three of them. All efforts to calm them down with remarks such as, "It's only a game!" and "It's only a mandala; it doesn't mean anything!" did not succeed—the emotional chaos was too great. The evening triggered the break-up of the new couple and the reunification of the original couple. It seemed that the mandala, or rather the spontaneous choice by the ex-wife, had shown them that there were still issues between them that were unresolved. Even though there was some suffering, the mandala game initiated a change in the lives of these three people. The two ex-partners returned to each other to finish something they had started, and the woman who had been left had to realize (and was finally able to) that the place at his side had not been hers to take in the first place. The mandalas had brought all this to light in their unique manner, which is so hard to explain. If only we let them, they can achieve amazing results. Not only do they say a lot about one's emotional life, they also reach deeper levels in people which are inaccessible by intellectual means alone.

Mandalas: Therapies and Diagnosis

Diagnosis with mandalas is a very popular subject, perhaps because we are virtually in love with the concept of diagnosis. The idea of knowing more than others, and in a way that others cannot understand, can be inspiring. Even though the examples that I described earlier are impressive in their own particular ways, there are far simpler and more reliable methods of diagnosis than mandalas. However, where emotions are concerned, there is no better method of therapy.

Traditional medicine shows quite clearly that we are much more fascinated with diagnosis than with therapy. It possesses an impressive array of diagnostic methods, but often, its therapeutic treatments seem to be stuck in the dark ages and are of a deplorable standard. Neurological patients find themselves being checked thoroughly for weeks, using the most advanced diagnostic methods, but when it comes to therapy, the question often is simply: steroids or no steroids? Many other areas of medicine also suffer from an over-emphasis on the diagnostic side.

Fortunately, it is the other way around with mandalas. They have great therapeutic value, even though we do not always know exactly why. Also, their use in therapy could not be simpler. Mandalas can be used by anyone, and they quickly turn patients into therapists. No qualification is necessary to become a mandala therapist. This may be somewhat disappointing for many people, since we usually tend to favor complicated subjects that require long years of training. It is their user-friendliness that makes mandalas so fascinating. In fact, if we take a closer look, we find that the best help is usually the most simple. Edward Bach, who developed his fascinating healing system of flower remedies from a variety of weeds and plants, untiringly emphasized the simplicity of his therapy.

Even if you only look at mandalas, you have already become your own therapist, and you should always try self-therapy before seeking a professional therapist. If you encourage others to color mandalas, you will pass on a wonderful method of therapy, but you should not exaggerate your own status as a therapist.

Coloring mandalas is often the best way to deal with emotional problems. With this in mind, it would be ideal if there were more mandala therapy and less traditional therapy. What speaks in favor of mandalas is the response they evoke in the people who use them. There are hardly any doctors who prescribe mandalas, and this is mainly because doctors do not take them seriously. Maybe they fear that their patients will not take them seriously if doctors recommend coloring mandalas twice a day. Thankfully, things are starting to change; occasionally, we now find a doctor who recommends coloring mandalas. Sadly as with many new spiritual ideas and philosophies which touch on medicine, doctors are often the last to follow a trend, and only after the trend has already been embraced by society.

If we consider that this kind of self-therapy comes virtually without any negative side effects, then there is really no other therapy to rival it. The only negative side effects that I have encountered were connected to the paperback edition of *Mandalas of the World*. In this edition, the mandalas are quite small. A person of an energetic, uninhibited nature can easily be exasperated by the constraints of such small designs. At the same time, too large a mandala can likewise cause anxiety. It seems that there are certain sizes for the mandalas which optimize their healing powers.

Diagnostic Advice

Even though I still do not regard mandalas as an established diagnostic method, I believe they may have some value—but we should beware of overemphasizing it. It would be all too easy to reverse the guidelines set by therapeutic treatments and then apply them to diagnostic problems.

Often, if people are aware of their centers, they tend to color mandalas from the center outward, freely entering the world that develops around them. In contrast, people who do not have basic trust and who are searching for themselves and their life paths will tend to color from the outside inward—these people will immediately encounter self-therapy and start their way to becoming more centered.

However, depending on people's moods, they may tend to confront their problems homeopathically, which will lead them directly to therapy. For example, introverted people will move away from the center, where they have been cocooned, while extroverted people will move toward the center. With this in mind, sometimes people are trying to avoid confronting their problems: in this case introverted people will retreat from the periphery (outside) to the center while coloring and extroverted people will—in accordance to their personalities—move from the inside to the outside of the mandala circle. Since homeopathic and allopathic treatments tend to alternate, we cannot arrive at a clear diagnosis this way. A detailed knowledge of all circumstances will always be necessary. Regardless, this does not usually pose a problem in mandala therapy. Usually, after periods of defensive, allopathic treatment, patients decide to change over to the homeopathic side, which is more helpful therapeutically.

People's abilities to deal with limits—whether they accept them readily or grudgingly, or defy them altogether, whether they allow themselves to make mistakes or are unable to forgive themselves an error—are revealed through coloring mandalas. Coloring mandalas can also reveal how people manage their time. If we take all of this into consideration, we may want to go a step further and include the choice of color and the preference of a certain shape into the diagnosis (you can find information on basic meanings of colors and shapes in *Mandalas of the World*).

From my point of view, the only really reliable way of making a responsible diagnosis lies in the interpretation of the basic principles which are at work. If you are familiar with the ten basic archetypes and how they express themselves in the world, then you will have a good basis of how to correctly interpret mandalas. Even though this subject goes far beyond the scope of this book, I would like to embrace it by using the mandalas. You will therefore encounter ten basic principle mandalas on your journey through this book. By coloring them, you will develop a feeling for the world of shapes, colors, and moods of each individual basic principle.

Therapy Experiences So Far

Reports from archaic cultures aside, which repeatedly told of ritual healings with the help of mandalas, we only had the positive testimony of C.G. Jung. Jung himself found mandalas helpful during the long crisis that followed his split from Freud. From then on, he held them in high regard. When they appeared in patients' dreams, he believed that they were either a cry for help from a soul in need, or a sign that a development had been completed. If a patient were to dream of mandalas after a long period of psychoanalysis, Jung felt it was a sign that the therapy was coming to an end. At the same time, he interpreted mandalas as both signals of desperation and as self-therapy for the souls of those psychotic patients to whom they were revealed. Mandalas could give stability to the lives of these people. Despite this apparent contradiction, there is no real problem because mandalas embrace entirety in all its facets and can, therefore, have contradictory meanings. The therapeutic effects of mandalas will always lean towards entirety and completeness.

For many years I have witnessed in our therapy center how mandalas can become an anchor for a soul in need. All of our reincarnation-therapy patients receive a copy of *Mandalas of the World* at the beginning of their therapy, and are encouraged to work with it as much as possible during the free time in their four-week stay, making it their own. Patients constantly report how helpful working with mandalas has been between difficult therapy sessions, especially for the integration of problematic issues. We now recommend coloring mandalas for integrating all kinds of difficult emotional experiences. A Persian proverb says, "Be patient, all things are difficult before they become simple." Coloring mandalas teaches a certain degree of patience and has a great influence on difficult things becoming simpler. By coloring, people come to accept the orderliness of the mandala, which seems to help their souls to create order. It is possible that mandalas intuitively help us to regain our perspective on what really matters in life. Since most experiences—and all disasters—take place on the periphery of the mandala and do not affect its center at all, the mandala can help to put everything in its proper place, which allows us to see again close up what is truly essential to us.

Patients who have difficult life circumstances tend to be more stable and receptive to therapy once they start coloring mandalas. Coloring makes therapy considerably easier for both sides—coloring mandalas is recommended for therapists as well—because patients enter therapy much more focused, good-humored, and happy. This is probably partly due to the fact that everybody, without exception, is good at coloring mandalas. It is almost impossible to ruin a mandala because of its round shape; it has a place for simply everything.

Everybody feels accepted by the mandala very quickly. Whatever colors one uses are okay, since they are readily integrated so the end result is always perfect. Mandalas may remind us of God's unconditional love, which is found in many religions. Whatever we do, we will not be abandoned by God's creation. The mandala will not abandon us either; it holds on to us with all our colors and crazy ideas and keeps us inside its circle.

Many patients immediately sense that they benefit from coloring these circular pictures, while in others, this realization comes a little bit later. Overall, there is remarkably little resistance to coloring mandalas as therapy, especially if the common misconception that "coloring is for children" is clarified at the very beginning. As soon as patients accept the old idea of *ora et labora* (pray and work) by which the Benedictine monks live, and enter into the ritual of coloring without ambition or boredom, everything usually takes its course and produces a well-rounded result.

When people color, they are constantly in motion; they go around in circles and always arrive at their destination. In Buddhism, this ritual is referred to as "doing as a symbol." Buddhists consider it very important to declare in advance that one does not intend to enjoy the fruits of such ritual labor. Another expression, which embraces this attitude is "the path is the goal." It is not important to arrive at a destination, and it is even less important to arrive there quickly.

It is very beneficial to continue the meditative coloring journey through the world of mandalas at home for as long as possible. By integrating mandalas into life after therapy, it becomes very clear that therapy is never really over until a patient feels liberated or finds God's heavenly kingdom in his own heart. I would like to stress again how effectively deeply moving emotional experiences can be integrated with the help of psychotherapy and, as well by coloring mandalas, particularly as these therapies will not let patients deny their experiences, but deal with them instead. There are many therapists who have combined these two therapies: for example, breathing therapists, who were trained by Stanislav Grof, often encourage their patients after a session to summarize the result and put it into a mandala. Not only do patients integrate the session's insights more easily, they also become aware of them on another level, since they have to make them fit into the perfect circle of the mandala. As they work through it once again, the whole experience becomes more rounded and more harmonious.

How Personality Influences the Direction of Coloring

Once I begin to know my patients, their therapeutic path can easily be controlled with the help of mandalas. Introverted patients who would like to become more outgoing, prefer to color mandalas from the inside to the edge. In the life pattern of the mandala this corresponds to the path from conception to midlife—the time of growth and development. Patients who are distracted, or who are fundamentally extroverted and tend to lose themselves in diversions, usually color from the outside toward the center. This path, which corresponds to the soul's way to home in the mandala, tends to help these patients become more centered. It also helps them to arrive at what is essential and to become closer to their own center.

One might argue that the results of such a far-reaching therapy program should not be overestimated, since coloring mandalas is only one of many available therapies. However, there are many accounts in which mandalas played a central role in therapy or even represented the main focus: the results were again extremely positive. As there are long waiting lists for reincarnation therapy, it is sometimes necessary to find an interim treatment for several often very difficult months. In these cases, the journey through the world of mandalas has often proven to be very beneficial, and in some cases has made psychotherapy unnecessary. Patients themselves sometimes say quite frankly, "I think coloring those mandalas really helped me a lot." They have helped themselves through self-therapy, which is—of course—one of the best forms of help and therapy.

We have similar accounts from former fasting patients who started to take responsibility and design their own courses of treatment. Frequently, they would put together an accompanying program consisting of coloring mandalas and guided meditation, which they had done in previous courses. They happily reported how they had the power to find themselves on their own and how they were able to recharge their batteries. They would often mention specifically how important mandalas had been in the process.

Even though findings like these have not been scientifically examined, I think it is now possible to generalize what I have discovered with my patients. This is not really surprising considering that a large number of my patients come to me not because they are sick, but because they have an interest in spirituality and a desire for emotional growth. Many accounts from therapists and an enormous number of letters from my readers confirm the healing effects of coloring and meditating with mandalas. It seems that even dealing with the background in theory of mandalas contributes to the healing process. There are many reasons for this, which we will encounter during the course of this book.

Mandalas and Soul Therapy

The mandala and its healing effects are too all-encompassing for us to analyze: they have some kind of effect on everything. But since we as human beings simply cannot deal with everything, it may be that medicine does not deal with the mandala. For years medicine was always searching for a cure-all. This was during a time when people still lived according to holistic ideas. Today, however, we tend to break everything down into its individual components; we analyze and search, and no longer expect to discover a cure-all. The mere concept just no longer fits our modern view of the world. For this reason, the mandala has a bad reputation with therapists who only think along scientific lines.

Actually, mandalas are a cure-all where emotional problems are concerned, and since a holistic view believes the physical is connected with the emotional, coloring mandalas is beneficial for almost any problem. Broad spectrum therapies seem suspicious to many people today who practice traditional medicine, but they are becoming very popular again with those who practice alternative therapies, such as fasting—which is recommended generally to all believers in the Bible, the Koran, the sutras of Buddhism, and other holy books.

Since we live in a society where people want to subdivide and label everything, we want likewise to subdivide and label the therapeutic effects of mandalas. However, it is important to be aware that this is an artificial step and to remain focused on the holistic aspect. Naturally, there are certain illnesses that respond particularly well to mandala therapy, but we must not conclude that mandalas have no bearing on any other complaints. It is quite obvious that mandala therapy is more effective with emotional problems than with physical problems.

With this in mind, we can easily see that a soul in disarray can rediscover itself in the mandala relatively well. Unfortunately, there are many reasons why the soul loses its way. Anything that is referred to as neurosis or psychosis is actually a soul that is on the wrong path. According to Freud, neuroses are so widespread that it is fairly impossible to find a person who has none whatsoever. We really have to consider almost all people neurotic.

The philosopher Hans Bluher referred to neuroses as rituals that have gone wrong, and this becomes very apparent when dealing with obsessive-compulsive neuroses. When a person washes his or her hands hundreds of times, it is likely a cleansing ritual that has gone wrong. As long as this ritual fails to work, the person will simply not be able to remove the "dirt." Even if the person's skin has almost been washed away, the soul does not see it— it is not the soul's reality. In cases like these, the best solution is to help the person find a functioning ritual.

The mere existence of neuroses should really be sufficient proof that the soul is much more powerful than the body. We have to understand, in the depths of our souls, that there are far more important, significant, and powerful elements than our intellect, which is greatly overvalued in this day and age. Anorexics intellectually know that they should really gain some weight out of physical necessity, but their (neurotic) life patterns will not allow them and will interfere at the next meal.

Another definition of neurosis can also be extended to some psychoses, namely that they are aberrations in time. This makes sense from the reincarnation therapy point of view. Often, neurotic behavior is the right behavior, but not in this time or under these circumstances. If we consider that mandalas take us to the center—into the "here and now"—we will find (with respect to the above definition) a plausible explanation for the good results that mandala therapy has achieved with neurotic disorders. Overall, working with mandalas, whether by coloring or meditating on them, encourages the gathering of one's emotions. While this is harmless with people who are just considered to be absent-minded, it hits harder with neurotics; however, focusing and moving closer to one's center brings great relief and is very helpful.

If patients suffer from multiple personalities, working intensively with mandalas will have a beneficial effect, supporting any psychotherapy the patient may be receiving. It seems that the circular pictures and their centering influence allow the patients to concentrate more easily on the central part of their subdivided personality. In times of distress these patients are literally "not quite there," because parts of their souls are actually tied up somewhere else. They find it extremely useful to be able to make their way through space and time, which seems to happen when they work with mandalas. Even in the most extreme cases of split personality, working with mandalas can greatly support psychotherapy. Patients who are usually referred to as "crazy" by others, are actually just lost in time and are disoriented spatially. It makes sense to help them rearrange the essential things in their lives and rediscover their place in space and time. They live in a world which—when looked at with the necessary sensitivity—reveals itself as entirely of its own.

Mandala therapy has also been beneficial in the treatment of cyclothymia, or manic-depressive disorder, which is characterized by extreme mood swings. These patients have lost their center, and anything that might bring them closer to it would be helpful. While psychotropic drugs can only cause the mood swings to be less extreme, mandalas create a link to the patient's center in both a real and a figurative sense. For instance, when we make a piece of pottery on the pottery wheel, the clay mandala has to be preserved at every turn and throughout every step of the work. The clay object grows, mandala by mandala, and every circular ring of clay has to be tightly joined to the previous mandala. The more ritually a person works the more strongly he or she will experience the symbolism of the mandala and the center.

Possibly the most far-reaching definition of neurosis is that the patient has lost sight of his or her path. Again, mandala therapy is a logical treatment for neuroses, since the mandala is the archetypal representation of a person's path through life. There is a chapter in this book on the subject that offers a variety of mandalas. When someone loses sight of his path, he can find it again in the mandala—even though we are unable rationally to explain why. There are special mandalas, such as the labyrinths shown extensively in *Mandalas of the World*, that are particularly devoted to the way through the maze of life, and they can, in a playful way, help people to regain what is essential.

With all these neurotic and even psychotic developments, where patients have lost their way and can no longer focus on their own center or on what is essential in life, the natural way to color mandalas is from the outside toward the center (at least this what should be encouraged). When patients contemplate the mandala or meditate on it, their gaze will automatically be drawn to the center; and by looking at the center of the mandala, they will automatically focus on their own centers, which is what they are aiming to recover.

Encouraging large parts of the population to work with mandalas could prevent emotional problems already mentioned, and even go beyond. Unfortunately, it is difficult to obtain objective results from preventative treatments; therefore, prevention is not highly regarded. It has almost been forgotten by traditional medicine, which nowadays seems to confuse it with early recognition. Our society holds a surgeon in much higher esteem and pays him considerably more than a health adviser, who can help to prevent many heroic surgeries. Sadly, we just do not know exactly what kind or how many.

At my healing center, coloring and mandala meditation therapy have been successful in treating all crises related to transitional periods in life (I have included some special mandalas in the book especially for these periods). When people are unable to clear the hurdle of transition, mandalas can show them, without putting too much pressure on them, that they have to go on with their lives. Coloring the mandalas in the appropriate direction allows people to gain a comforting insight into the hopelessness of their existing life patterns. People appear to sense intuitively, when they are coloring mandalas over a long period of time, that the pattern is preordained, and that they only need to accept it, but not change it. Resistance to an impending stage of development disappears while the person circles around the center, and it is replaced with the insight that this development is necessary.

Dying is one of our most taboo subjects, and yet it appears as the *central* point in the mandala of life. What is more, the aspect of release becomes the main focus and replaces all of the usual horror visions of death. In fact, the increase of all kinds of depression can be ascribed to our collective denial of death. The subject of dying becomes an unresolved issue because it is not sufficiently dealt with on a conscious level. People suffering from depression think about dying, but this usually takes the form of suicidal thoughts. Instead of pondering the question "rope or bullet, poison or gas," these people should reconcile themselves with the idea of dying through religion or philosophy. For some cultures this attitude is a given: the Tibetans, for instance, do not know depression as we understand it. Even dealing with this subject on a subconscious level while coloring helps to reduce fear. Mandalas confront us with the finiteness of our lives in a way that we find bearable. If you want to deal with the subject of death, color the mandala from the outside toward the center, so that it becomes clear how everything results in the point of solution and release.

Mandala coloring therapy also helps to treat crises pertaining to the midpoint in life, which frequently triggers depression. In mandalas, the midpoint in life appears as the circumference of the circle, or as a borderline. Through coloring and meditation, this transition becomes accessible in a non-intellectual fashion—so typical of mandalas—and it manifests itself as an essential, irreplaceable part of the pattern and of life. If you want to deal with your "midlife crisis," you should color the mandala from the inside out. This will help you to become more aware intuitively that the borderline is finite and that there is no alternative to moving forward.

In order to achieve the best results in dealing with life crises, the general rule is to color in the same direction that you are currently taking in life. For other crises relating to major transitions, the mandala also offers valuable help, which—although it cannot be grasped intellectually—manifests itself very clearly. This also applies to other crises, such as problems in relationships, work, and especially one's spiritual life.

If we consider that mandalas help us to achieve inner calm and to focus on what is essential, then we are able to understand their effects more easily—often, in times of crisis, it is inner calm and focus that seem to be temporarily lost.

Physical Ailments and Mandala Therapy

After 20 years of working in psychosomatic medicine, I have no doubt whatsoever about the constant interaction between the body and the soul. For this reason, I believe that psychosomatic diseases and ailments only affect a person's soul, or awareness. Therefore, emotional or psychological issues always cause physical ailments. Mandalas can be used to help them, but it might not immediately suggest itself as an option as it does for psychological complaints.

Cancer, a disease that establishes itself very deeply inside the physical body, has a very obvious connection to losing one's path through life, which makes mandala therapy a very good treatment for it. Due to their illness, cancer patients especially are encouraged to attempt self-realization. They should learn to accept their path and stop passing life by. The term "normopathy," which is used in this context by Wolf Buntig, highlights the negative side of this overly cautious emotional pattern that can develop into a dangerous disease. Cancer patients need to learn to lead their own, self-determined lives, to be extremely enthusiastic about their way to self-realization, and to tackle it with courage. Only the mandala can teach them how to decide between the pre-ordained archetypal patterns and their individual possibilities of influencing them.

All paths are different, but they all eventually lead to death. The attempt to change this fact is completely futile and will lead to despair—the same thing will happen also when we do not utilize our individual paths. Since mandalas—in their easy and playful manner—help to achieve clarity, the ability to differentiate, and a better relationship with one's own path through life, mandala therapy has become indispensable in supporting the treatment of cancer patients.

Cancer aside, there are many other diseases that can benefit from the calming and focusing influence of mandalas, even if they are used to simply distract the patient. In these cases, mandalas are not used to their full power, but are still effective. For whatever reason they are used, mandalas always bring the full spectrum of their—sometimes seemingly magical—possibilities.

Channeling Energies with Mandalas

There is no scientifically logical explanation for this, but everything seems to indicate that mandala therapy also contributes to harmonizing the flow of energy. As a perfect, rotationally symmetric figure—to use geometric terminology—the mandala communicates the highest level of harmony. We do not know how this is transmitted to the person coloring the mandala or meditating on it, but we are certainly able to witness it. In societies that still consciously live with mandalas, people do know how this happens. The wise woman or the medicine man simply takes some colored sand and other natural materials from which the mandala was made and places it on the person who is in need of healing. Thus, the mandala, together with its harmony and its energy, is transmitted to the patient. It may seem like hocus-pocus to us, but it works remarkably well in most cases and often much better than our tranquilizers, which simply block emotions.

The phenomenon of transmitting order from the mandala becomes more understandable when we look at it with the psyche in mind. People who have regained their emotional balance have a more harmonious flow of energy. Studies in neuro-psycho-immunology found that mood swings, for example, have an impact on the human blood count. It makes sense that we use mandalas to maintain a healthy psyche.

If we look at the subtle energy systems known by ancient cultures, such as Indian, Chinese, and Tibetan, for thousands of years, they help us to determine the influence that mandalas have. Chakras, long recognized by Hindus as the most important energy nodes in the body, take the form of mandalas—at least people who are aware of them have represented them as mandalas. Therefore—if only on the basis of the law of resonance—mandala work should activate one's own energy centers in a positive manner. We will look at the practical side of chakras in a later part of this book.

As coloring mandalas restores order on all emotional levels, it would be fair to assume that it also supports order on all levels of the physical body.

Accessing Inner Sources of Energy Through Mandalas

It is a strange phenomenon that mandalas can actually give patients strength and energy, and we can really comprehend it only by drawing analogies. People with a materialistic attitude will find it hard to understand, but those who practice moving closer to the secret of the mandala's center will usually experience it. There seems to be a special power that resides at the center of all things, and once you have experienced it, you will notice its effects and feel them within yourself. However, you will not be able to comprehend this power on an intellectual level.

Real power lies at the center of things. A person who rests securely in the knowledge of his center cannot be knocked over by physical force. We can see this in Far-Eastern martial artists. Mandalas can help us establish a relationship with our own center, helping us to access the power that lies within. This power is called "core energy" or "central force" by Gestalt therapists. As much as we know about physics and the enormous forces in the nucleus of an atom, we are relatively unaware of our own emotional "nuclear energy." But with the help of the mandala, we are at least able to enjoy it once in a while.

There is evidence that, due to its shape and a person's readiness to be drawn into it, the mandala can actually put people in a trance when they are meditating on it or even just coloring it. This becomes especially clear when meditating on mandalas such as the one on page 200, relating to chaos theory, which put extra emphasis on the magnetic pull of the center. The pull of the center focuses our concentration which in turn sharpens our awareness—similar to a magnifying glass which concentrates rays of light into a single point. At this point of concentration in the center, unexpected forces come into play and things become possible that would be unimaginable in normal awareness. This may be part of the secret of healing trances. In archaic societies, healing rituals were mostly conducted in a trance. It seems that a person's awareness, if it is concentrated, has the tendency to encourage healing processes in the right places with amazing power. Another possible explanation is that our self-healing powers are activated as soon as we switch off our intellectual awareness. Many experiences from psychotherapy, as well as from natural healing, support this theory. When a person is in a trance, there is justified hope that the "inner physician" will be able to use his powers to help himself.

The mandala has been very successful over the last decade, especially among the more spiritually inclined. Another secret of this success may lie in the fact that the intellect gently withdraws, almost unnoticeably, without causing any concern. The intellect has become so predominant in our industrial societies that some people gratefully accept any opportunity to gain some distance from its dictatorship.

Coloring Mandalas as Play Therapy

Unfortunately, we are not really used to the idea that therapy can be easy, playful, and fun. It is typical that although my book, *Mandalas of the World*, was created to accompany therapies, the mandala wave started in spiritual circles and not in the world of therapy. Following *Mandalas of the World*, this book can be considered a second attempt at a therapy book, although I was very excited about the response from my first book within spiritual circles.

As a doctor, I am still very interested in the healing quality of mandalas and the idea of mandalas supporting other therapies. Mandalas are almost ingeniously simple. People in need of healing can work with them at their own leisure. They are also fun to color and give us a sense of joy—fun and a zest for life are probably the most underestimated subjects in modern therapy. Only very gradually are we seeing the beginnings of such treatments as "clown therapy" in some children's hospitals. It has been shown that a clown who visits sick children in their wards not only distracts them from their illness, but also puts them in a happier frame of mind that significantly improves the healing process.

One of the latest developments is laughter research, which is taken quite seriously. Its results are very encouraging, as was to be expected. Scientists could have saved themselves some research because we have known for a long time that laughing is good for us. It refreshes the heart and keeps us young.

People have also said for a long time that "round is sound." After the rediscovery of mandalas in our society, we no longer need to apply this wisdom exclusively to our bodies. Round is sound and whole, and that, of course, is a lot of fun. A zest for life is something so natural that it just flows forth from the pattern of life without any help. We simply need to tune into it, and the mandala may be the easiest way to do this in a ritual manner. Patients today show a lack of zest for life. If we could infuse them with zest, then we would be doing it already. But since this is not possible, we should at least encourage it through therapy, where patients teach themselves to enjoy life by coloring in circles and meditating on the center of the mandala, which as you know already corresponds to their own centers.

One would think that it should be fairly easy to integrate the coloring of mandalas into artistic therapies. Artists, however, usually find it extremely difficult to accept pre-ordained structures; they place creativity above everything else. As important as creativity is, painting freely is no match for coloring mandalas as far as its healing properties are concerned. Of course art is a wonderful way of dealing with problems. But the mandala seems to address much more central areas in patients, pre-school children, and pupils.

Mandalas: the Path to Perfection

Each and every mandala is perfect and represents perfection. Since we do not deal with this ultimate goal of human development sufficiently, neither within religion nor philosophy, mandalas create a wonderful balance. Whether we like to admit it or not, when we color mandalas, we are developing perfection.

The link between the spiritual path and medicine's desire to heal lies in the common goal of perfection. Originally, medicine, like meditation, aimed to lead patients to their center. The fact that both words share the same root may serve us as guarantee, even though modern medicine seems almost to have lost sight of this original goal. Even perfect health in body, mind, and soul—to which traditional medicine is still committed today—ultimately means being in one whole and perfect piece: self-realization, liberation, and enlightenment are different words for this same concept.

The mandala is a representation and symbol of perfection, and it might be able to bring traditional medicine a little closer to its original goal. Quite obviously it rekindles in people who work with it a desire for self-realization and perfection. It is therefore understandable that it triggers different reactions in different situations. Under the influence of the mandala, people tend to integrate whatever is lacking from the whole and from perfection. If a young person undergoing puberty lacks the courage to take an important step, the mandala will center his energies onto the task. If somebody suffering from depression finds it difficult to accept death, the mandala will make it easier by steering the person's subconscious towards the center of the mandala. As the mandala embraces everything, everybody will find his own topic within it and will learn to integrate it into the greater context of his life—how this happens is not yet known. If you are coloring mandalas, you have embarked on your path, although every person is at a different stage in life and experiences different things.

Mandala Rituals

When working with mandalas becomes a ritual, the better the therapeutic effect will be. It would go far beyond the scope of this book to discuss at length the subject of rituals, but below are some steps for creating your own mandala ritual with the most harmonious energies possible, in order to make it the most effective:

1. A ritual lives particularly through the awareness with which it is carried out. Therefore, it is advisable to remain silent or be by yourself.

2. The effect of a ritual is mainly conveyed through a pattern of vibrations. It is a good idea to create conditions for conducting the ritual which will allow you to follow these vibrations on different levels. It is also good to play music that touches your soul, such as mantra chants. You could also use a scent that makes you more responsive. Correct lighting is important as well, as is the correct general atmosphere.

3. Everything is helpful which concentrates your senses on the ritual, in addition to the centering effect of the mandala itself. The more concentrated the ritual, the more impressive its effect on the soul will be.

4. The ritual should mean something to you. If this is not yet the case, you should try to personalize it accordingly. To begin with, you could make this book utterly your own and treat it with respect and love as you start your path to the center.

5. If you are using a mandala for an important occasion, it is a good idea to choose the place carefully for the mandala ritual and the amount of time—of course the mandala itself will have a bearing on the quality of place and time.

6. Achieving inner calmness through meditation before the ritual will reinforce its effect.

7. The best attitude for coloring is one of contemplation, not one that emphasizes performance or efficiency. Allowing plenty of time therefore is a prerequisite for a deep experience.

Using Mandalas in Education

Ultimately, the use of mandalas in education cannot be separated from their use in therapy. The healing effects which caused teachers to let their pupils color mandalas, completely correspond to those experienced in psychotherapy. Children who were coloring mandalas became calm immediately and tended to concentrate better on their work. This is probably the key aspect for educators. Quiet is always necessary for learning, but it is hard to achieve through disciplinary measures that are never really satisfactory.

Over the years we have had many reports from teachers, especially from those at special education schools, who confirmed the wonderful effects of simple mandala exercises and wanted to know how they came about. The mandala is especially helpful for children with special needs. If they can hold a pencil, they will achieve a beautiful result because the mandala's perfect circle easily absorbs all kinds of difficulties. In the same way that it reconciles different parts of a rebellious personality, it also combines conflicting pencil strokes into perfect harmony. The mandala is also well suited for the so-called "difficult pupils," because the circle, which absorbs everything, gives them an opportunity to channel their frustration or anger. Coloring mandalas has even shown good results for children whose fine motor skills are underdeveloped.

Some teachers have even gone as far as letting their pupils color a mandala before tests to help them calm down, concentrate better, and gather their thoughts. Apparently, the results are impressive, not just with the working atmosphere during the exam, but also with exam results. Some teachers even encourage their pupils, after each page of math problems, to color a mandala on the opposite page, as order is obviously an important aspect in mathematics.

Maybe the nicest aspect of working with mandalas in education is that the mandala in itself is fun. If we consider that—besides and even before imparting knowledge—the main goal of education consists in helping pupils to develop and establish their personalities and to guide them in finding their way through life, then we might start to suspect that we are still underestimating mandalas in this area.

A Summary of the Opportunities that We Gain from Mandalas

Mandalas enable us:

- To learn to cope with limits, and to accept those that are necessary
- To shape the space that exists between limitations
- To find quiet and to rest within ourselves

Mandalas deal with:

- Relaxed focus and concentration
- Orientation within our pattern of life
- A better integration of experiences
- Learning to be responsive to a pattern
- Peak experiences—in the sense of experiencing unity
- Developing a more rounded personality
- Gaining strength from our own centers

The Mandala as the Basic Pattern of Creation: A Journey from the Microcosm to the Macrocosm

Even the more materialistically inclined will be able to see that the mandala is the most important pattern—or symbol—in our world since everything in the material world is made of mandalas. Atoms are mandalas, regardless of whether we look at Niels Bohr's model of the atom or the newer models by quantum physicists (both represent the whirling dance of electrons around the nucleus of the atom). In the depths of the microcosm—the smallest things we can imagine today—we always encounter nothing but mandalas. There is strong evidence that we should picture the elementary particles (neutrons, protons, and electrons) as mandalas. Even the quarks, the most recently found components of the atom, that make up protons, can be seen as mandalas.

The energy dance around the center of the atom resembles a dance around a void because the nucleus of an atom is so tiny that most the atom's insides actually consist of empty space. If we were to enlarge an atom to the size of the largest church in Christendom, St. Peter's Cathedral in Rome, then the nucleus would only be the size of a speck of dust. Yet, everything revolves around it.

Unfortunately, even today, we are unable to take photographs of atoms because they are much too small; but modern physics has managed to make them visible. The effects of atoms can be photographed, in a manner of speaking, by using x-rays. Via the tip of a platinum pin, x-rays are transmitted onto atoms, where they are reflected, creating the pattern shown on the opposite page: an expanse of mandalas. This is the deepest we can delve into the microcosm using our "technical eyes."

A Field of Atom Mandalas

Microcosm = Macrocosm

Moving from the smallest things perceivable to the greatest, such as our galaxy, the Milky Way, we encounter innumerable mandalas on all different levels. This path through our creation is a path through nature, which surrounds us and of which we consist. When we move through creation by coloring and meditating with mandalas, it is our goal to reconcile ourselves with this universal pattern so that we can thrive within it. Since we find the same pattern everywhere, inside and outside of us, we will be less afraid of the unknown and become more familiar with the world. Man represents a small world of his own, which will take on enormous dimensions once we examine it more closely.

Microcosm and Macrocosm

Atom Mandalas and Cell Mandalas

All the cells in our body, as well as those in animals and plants, are mandalas. Even though their shapes vary, they all live according to the same mandala principle. A cell's nucleus is at rest most of the time. From this restfulness, it controls all events around it: everything revolves around this center.

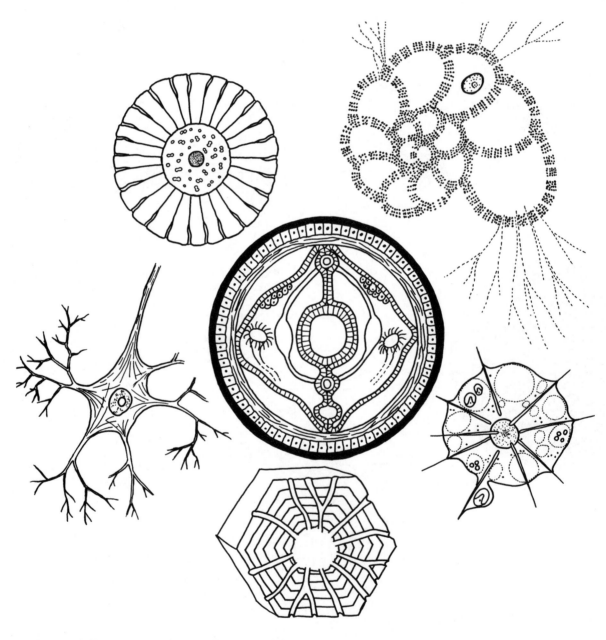

Above, different mandala cells from different organisms are centered around the cross-section of an earthworm.

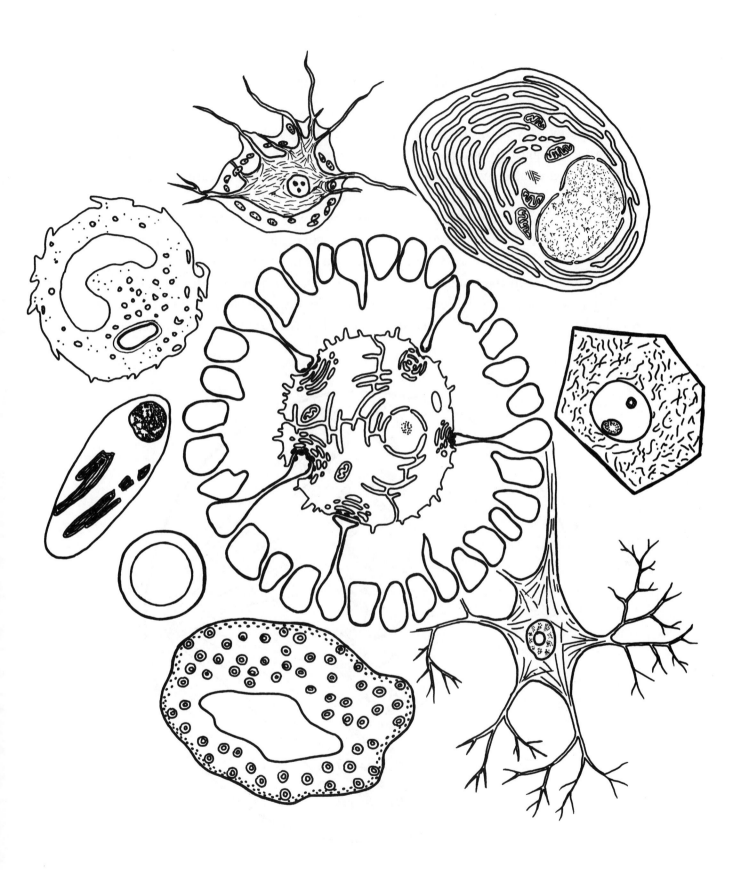

Different Types of Cells in the Human Body

Mandala Analogies

On our journey we will constantly encounter similarities between the microcosm and the macrocosm. The journey into space, i.e., the macrocosm, and the examination of the inside of a cell or even an atom will constantly make us aware of their similarities. The big, empty expanse of the universe corresponds to the wide and empty space within an atom. If, however, we encounter something on our journeys, it will almost certainly be a mandala.

If we look at cell division inside a nucleus, we will come across the characteristic spindles that control the division and the multiplication of new cells. In the macrocosm, geographers have imposed the same spindle pattern on the earth by introducing the meridian and the equator for degrees of longitude and latitude, respectively. It is doubtful that they were thinking of the world of the microcosm, but this was the most logical system to use.

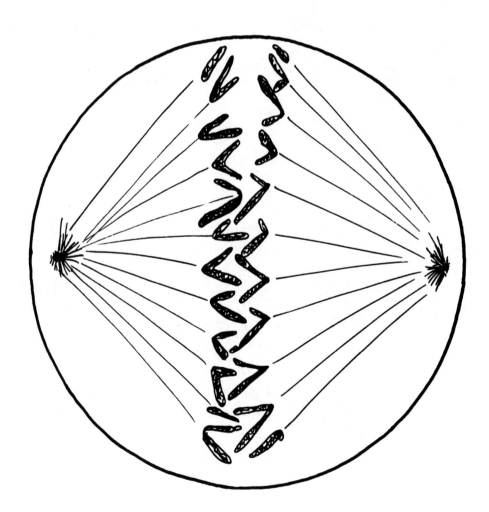

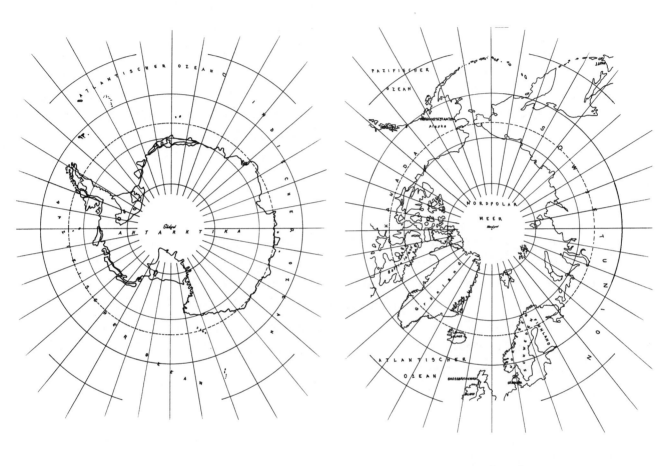

South Pole   *North Pole*

41

The Mandala World of Crystals

If you have seen in silent prayer
How the soul of the earth fashions crystals,
If you have seen the flame in the growing seed
And death in life and birth in decay,
If you have found brothers in men and beasts,
And if you recognized in the brother, the brother and God,
Then you will celebrate at the table of the holy grail
Communion with the messiah of love.
You will search and you will find, just like God said,
The way to the lost paradise.

MANFRED KYBER

Just as organic life forms cells out of atom mandalas, the inorganic world uses atoms to create all kinds of crystals. Grown inside the earth for millions of years, crystals develop according to amazingly regular designs that can often be traced back to mandalas. Just as man is made up of billions and billions of mandala-shaped cells, rocks and mountains are made of crystalline structures. The easiest way to visualize the image of a growing crystal may be by looking at stalagmites and stalactites. Of course, both types of rock formation show mandalas in their cross-sections.

At the center is a natural crystal surrounded by gemstones cut in various ways, which are almost always mandalas.

The Two Sides of Crystals

Like everything in creation, mandalas have two sides. While there are many beautiful crystals that bring us great joy, there are also many that are not very pleasant at all. Some, such as the crystals of uric acid which cause gout, can even bring pain.

Uric Acid Crystal

Mountain Ranges Made of Animal Mandalas

If the basic substance of a mountain range does not consist of crystalline components, it may still consist of mandalas, as is the case with limestone mountains. Over billions of years, these mountains grow from tiny little petrified-shell lime structures—themselves mandalas from the realm of water. The coral reefs in the ocean grow in a similar manner. In their cross-section, the coral branches are all mandalas.

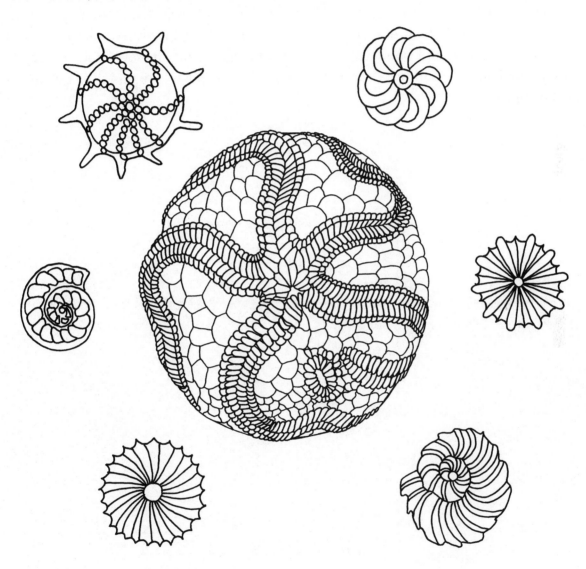

The World of Water: A World of Mandalas

Each drop of water is not just a universe within itself, it is also a mandala. Even billions of mandala waterdrops combined, though their origin is no longer visible, still carry this pattern inside and reveal it at every possible opportunity. When you throw a stone into water, you create a very vivid mandala that spreads out over the entire surface of the water—no matter how large the body of water is. It may be that the final extent of this dynamic mandala becomes so subtle that it is invisible to our eyes. Every time water is set in motion, it reveals billions of its little mandala drops. This is particularly beautiful in a rainbow, which is created when white sunlight is broken up into its seven rainbow colors through millions of raindrops. The rainbow is a half mandala composed of billions of small mandalas.

This is the result of a single waterdrop mandala that falls into water and immediately creates a crown of mandalas, no two ever the same.

Our Daily Water

Water is even more important for survival than our daily bread. Water, like all other liquids, loves to take on mandala shapes at every opportunity. Water forms the most unusual and attractive shapes when it flows, be it through all those miles of pipe that transport water in and out of our houses, or the arteries and veins of our bodies, which are all mandala-shaped in their cross-sections. The illustrations on the following pages show how water always forms mandala shapes when it flows.

Nature chooses its shapes from an unimaginable wealth of possibilities and ensures that there is an order to it all: mandalas. Our blood flows through our bodies according to strict rules, and mandala-shaped blood cells conform to these regulations.

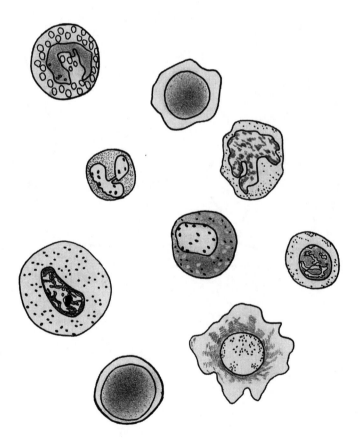

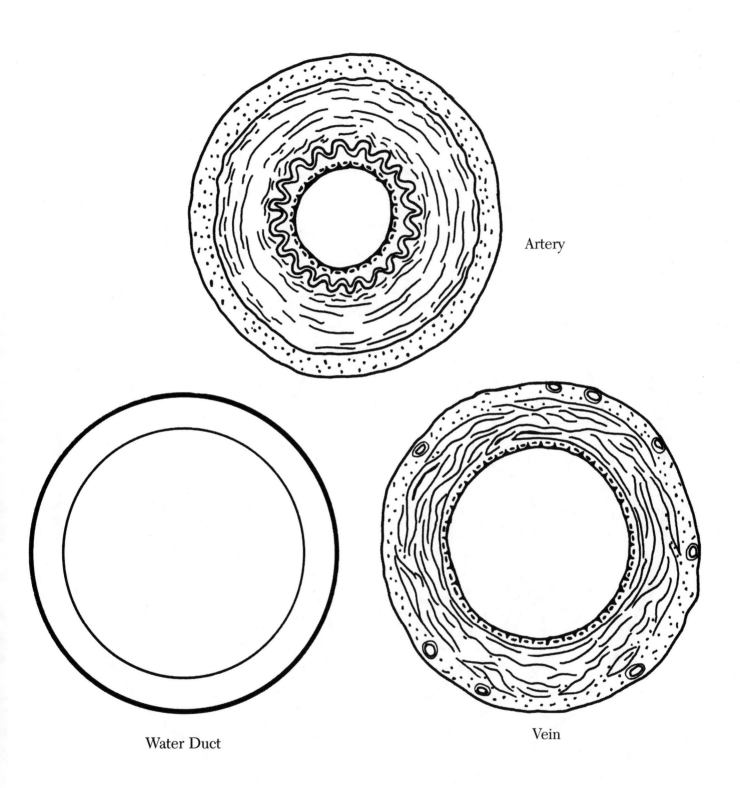

Artery

Water Duct

Vein

The Water of Life in Its Different Ducts

49

Duct

Duct

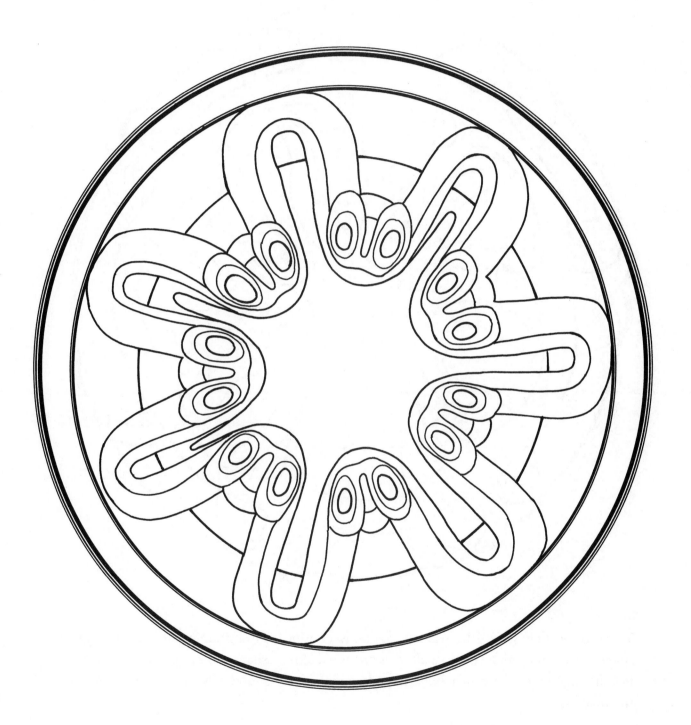

Duct

These three flow shapes have been randomly chosen from a literally infinite number of shapes. They may give you a small idea of the wealth of shapes in nature, which goes far beyond anything we can imagine. They also show nature's tendency to base everything on the mandala.

The Mandala Whirlpool

The familiar sight of water forming a whirlpool is actually quite an amazing phenomenon, yet we still do not understand how they form. We only know from experience that there is a great secret at the center of the mandala and that strange forces are at work in these whirlpools. In our hemisphere, the direction of the spin in a whirlpool is always clockwise, but nobody knows why. The English physicist Thompson, who became famous as Lord Kelvin, built a whole physical concept of the world on spiral vortexes. However, it fell into oblivion, just like the groundbreaking research by the Austrian private scholar Viktor Schauberger, who investigated the secret of the water vortex on a practical level.

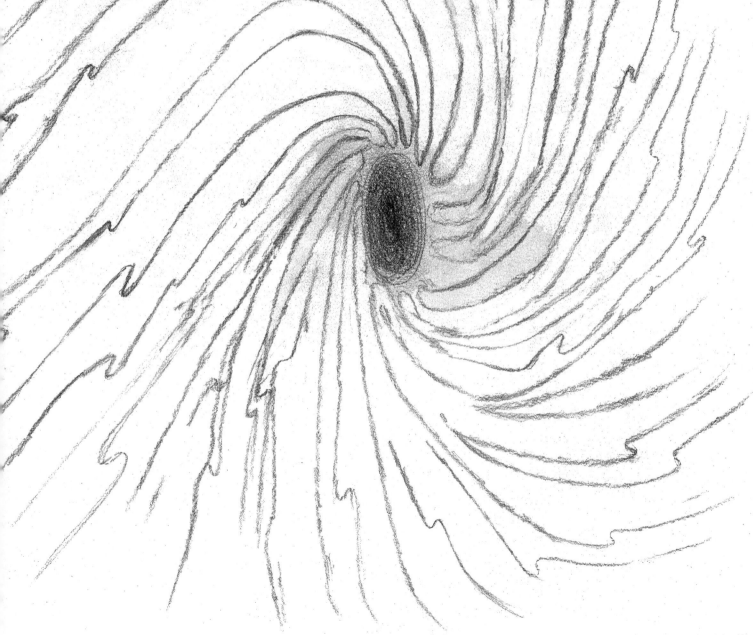

Unusual Mandalas

Other liquids have a tendency to form a spherical mandala. Almost all solids can be made liquid; it is just a question of circumstances, especially temperature. Glass can be made out of the crystals of quartz sand and then shaped through the skills of the glass blower into wonderful mandala-shaped drops. We like to enjoy such fragile, colorful mandalas as balls on the Christmas tree, which during one of the longest nights of the year has symbolized our hope for the rebirth of the light—since pre-Christian times. From God's point of view, the Christmas tree is definitely a mandala.

But it is not only quartz sand that, as glass, flows into mandala shapes. Liquid stone, too, can flow down from the crater of a volcano in the form of lava. Depending on the temperature, metals can flow as well. Ultimately, all matter displays a tendency towards forming mandala-shaped drops or spheres. The physical reason is obvious: the sphere, or the mandala, is the shape that can accommodate the greatest volume in the smallest space. The mandala shape develops as a result of surface tension. This becomes apparent when we look at mercury, the only metal that is liquid at room temperature. Given the opportunity, it divides into thousands of little mandala spheres of all sizes. Once we bring all of them back together, they readily return to the shape of a larger sphere; but they always maintain the shape of a mandala.

The Christmas Tree Mandala

The Christmas tree, which never loses its leaves, represents an evergreen ray of hope in a world of winter where the light slowly dies, only to be reborn ritually during the longest night of the year. It is a symbol much older than Christianity. The druids would put lights and cakes on a fir tree as a symbol of never-ending life. The Christmas tree will almost certainly remain with us, but I am not so sure about other Christmas-related accessories. For instance, there are fewer and fewer nativity scenes under our Christmas trees. Below is a Christmas tree with mandala-shaped balls, seen from a heavenly perspective.

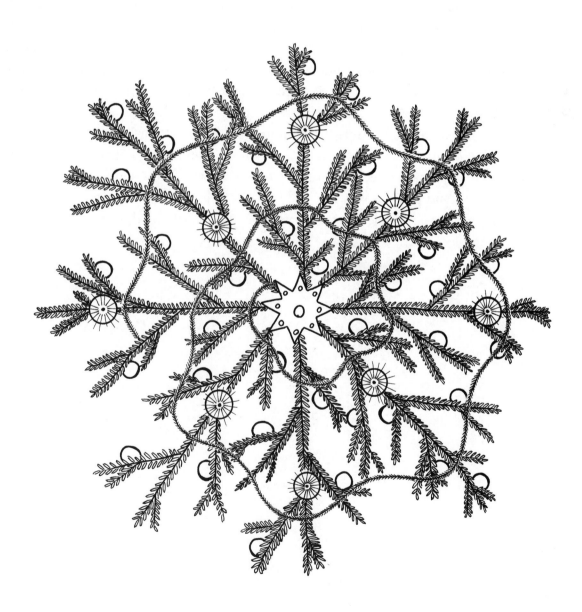

Living Off the Mandala World of Water

As far as liquids are concerned, water remains the one great wonder that dominates everything. Maybe someday it will tell us how it stores the patterns of homeopathic remedies and retains them beyond the material realm, or how it absorbs the healing effects of Bach flowers. Water is the most important substance on earth simply because all life originates in it, both in the evolutionary and personal senses. All mammals, including man, develop in amniotic fluid, which actually has a similar composition to the primeval ocean.

Like most living creations on this planet, we have not left the water entirely. We have taken it onto dry land in the cells of our bodies, so our bodies mainly consist of water. At every opportunity, we return to the water's edge and to the water itself. We love to bathe from early childhood on, and this love rarely seems to diminish. The closer the water temperature is to that of the amniotic fluid in the mother's womb, the happier we are. When people freely float in thermal water that is at body temperature, they frequently experience the same feelings of bliss that they had back in their mother's wombs. It is perfectly clear that our ties to our original home, the water, remain intact throughout our lives.

The smallest creatures that live in water and consist of almost nothing else stand at the beginning of the food chain, which secures life on our planet. They remind us that all life originated in water, and that humans are made up of at least two-thirds water. In the analogy of the microcosm and macrocosm, more than two-thirds of the earth mandala is covered in water.

Exercise: Return to the Water Mandala

For swimmers: Put a pair of flotation devices around your ankles and lie in still, thermal water that is at body temperature. Let go. You will notice your body being very stable in the water, so that you can even relax your neck. If you are breathing calmly from your center, you will soon feel your breathing rocking you gently with its rhythm. Do not worry; you will not get any water in your mouth or nose. You can even let go further and let your closed eyes be covered by a thin layer of water. If you open your eyes a tiny bit, you will see the world above you—due to the refraction of the light on the water's surface—as one big mandala. You can go even further and let your arms and legs drift apart, becoming a mandala yourself: a five-pointed star mandala that floats in the water.

Soon you will start to feel weightless and, if the water is warm enough, you will also experience a sensation of boundlessness. This wonderful situation may give rise to peak experiences, which means you can experience unity (with everything). There may be oceanic feelings of vast expanses, or feelings of ecstasy and exhilaration. Something in you may be reminded of your early days in the amniotic fluid of your mother's womb, where you also floated weightlessly and felt warm and secure. This is the time when we develop basic trust, which becomes the foundation for self-confidence later on in life. This exercise can actually, through the experience of unity, increase your basic trust and with it, your self-confidence. Once you have done this several times, you can try it without the flotation devices, since practically all men and women can float without aid—just the way God made them.

The feelings of freedom and regression—in the sense of returning to one's origin—are difficult to describe, but easily experienced. At any rate, you will soon be in your element: water, your element and your original home.

A Freely Floating Organism that Lives in Water

The Waterdrop Mandala

The ocean contains many mandalas of all sizes and at all depths. There are billions of plankton mandalas, which mark the beginning of life, as they stand at the beginning of the food chain. They lead us back through the history of evolution to the very beginnings of life.

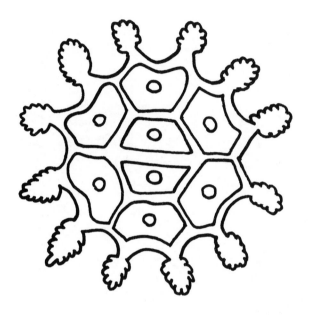

Plankton

Fascinating Mandalas from the Ocean

Even larger water creatures, such as shells, have retained the mandala structure, which may be why children love to collect them. Whether it is snails, shells, or starfish, collecting them means collecting mandalas. If a shell is broken and the mandala destroyed, it has lost its fascination.

A Particularly Stunning Shell

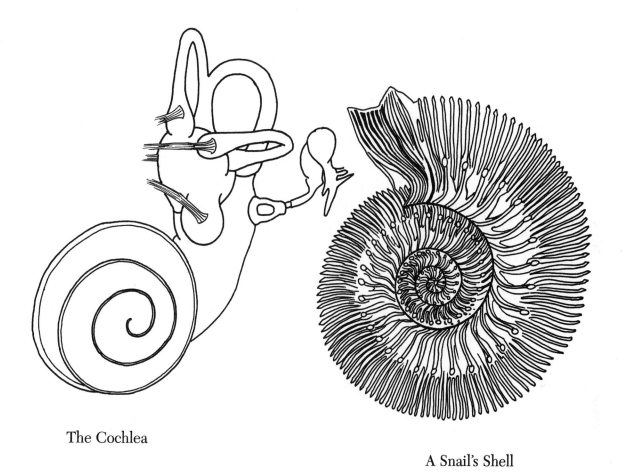

The Cochlea

A Snail's Shell

The spiral shape of the snail can also be found in the cochlea of our inner ear. Not only do we carry the water of the primeval sea in every cell of our bodies, but the solid structures within our bodies also remind us of the origin of all life and of the close relationship of mandala structures in both the microcosm and the macrocosm. We, as human beings, are part of this world and also carry the world inside us. If only we started noticing this fact, we could care better for the inner and outer worlds and would no longer need to torture our cochleae with so much noise.

The Magical World of Snowflakes

Before we leave the world of water behind, I would like to mention one of its most amazing manifestations within nature: the magical world of snowflakes. If we consider that no two snowflakes are alike, we can gain an insight into the unimaginable wealth of shapes and ideas within nature. While you are coloring this snow flurry, you may realize that this phenomenon of immense variety within a set framework is not limited to snowflakes alone.

While you are coloring these snowflakes in appropriate cool shades of white and blue, your respect for the wealth of possibilities within nature may grow even further. We will never outdo her, but to show respect to her and every single one of her innumerable snowflakes should be one of our commandments.

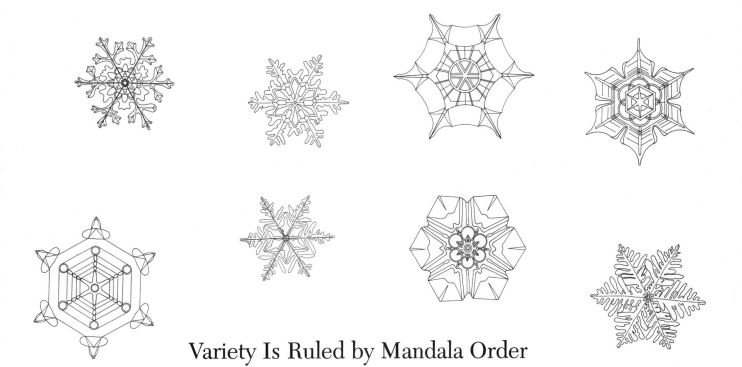

Variety Is Ruled by Mandala Order

Even though there are no two identical snowflakes, they are all formed according to the same principles. Not only are they all mandalas, they are also little individual six-pointed stars. With their regular hexagram structure, they bear witness to the enormous sense of order within Mother Nature. And just as there are no two identical snowflakes, there are no two persons who are identical; yet they all follow the same mandala pattern along their paths through life.

A snow flurry of these unique crystals can remind us that we as humans, despite our individuality, still follow the same inner pattern: the mandala. It is found in every cell and every atom, and we also follow it through the greater pattern of our lives. Not even identical twins are exactly the same—their mandala fingerprints are different.

Flower Mandalas in the Spring and Fruit Mandalas in the Fall

As we emerge from the realm of water and return to Mother Earth's dry crust, we naturally remain within the realm of mandalas. The diversity which we find in the mandala garden of blossoms, reminds us of the great variety of snowflakes flurrying through the air. Like the stars in the nighttime sky, blossoms sparkle in the sunshine on earth. The great majority of flowers have based their blossoms on the mandala, and their lovely star-shapes have successfully attracted insects for millions of years.

The rose is not just the queen of flowers; practically all our fruit trees belong to the rose family, such as apple, pear, cherry, plum, and all berry-bearing shrubs, from raspberry to blackberry to currant.

The Secret of the Center

The secret of the mandala lies in its center. Some flowers hide their centers bashfully with their petals, like the rose on the previous page, while others show them off almost shamelessly, like the poppy pictured below.

It is not just the flower's secret that lies in the center; it is also the secret of all mandalas. With flowers it is simply more obvious. At the center of a blossom are its reproductive organs: the pistil and the stamen. For the simple purpose of attracting insects, flowers have developed magnificent colors and shapes, as well as a seductive scent. The reproductive organs, however, contain the secret of polarity, the opportunity to make two into one or to revoke the division that runs through creation.

In India, the lotus flower has the same significance as the rose in the western world. We will see it again when we look at chakras. It can be found in most Hindu mandalas.

The Human Being Within the Mandala: Mandalas Within the Human Being

Leonardo da Vinci represented man as a five-pointed star, which is a mandala.

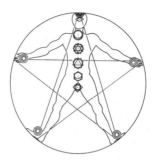

We do not just carry, as has already been described, the mandala signature in every atom, but also in every cell in our body. Some star-shaped nerve cells show this very clearly, but all cells, in general, show the same dance around the middle as in the atom.

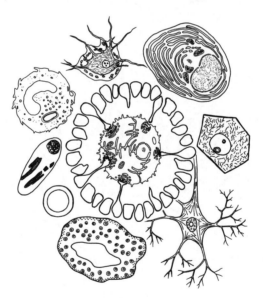

It goes further: a cell's nucleus is also an almost perfect mandala, which stores at its center the genetic information of humans, animals, and plants. As with flowers, we find that the secret is hidden in the center. Knowledge is encoded in the double helixes of the DNA, which is still not entirely understood today. There is justified suspicion that each cell nucleus also stores a large part of our evolutionary history. Our illustration shows the spiral pattern in the nucleus of an immature blood cell.

The Nucleus of an Immature Blood Cell

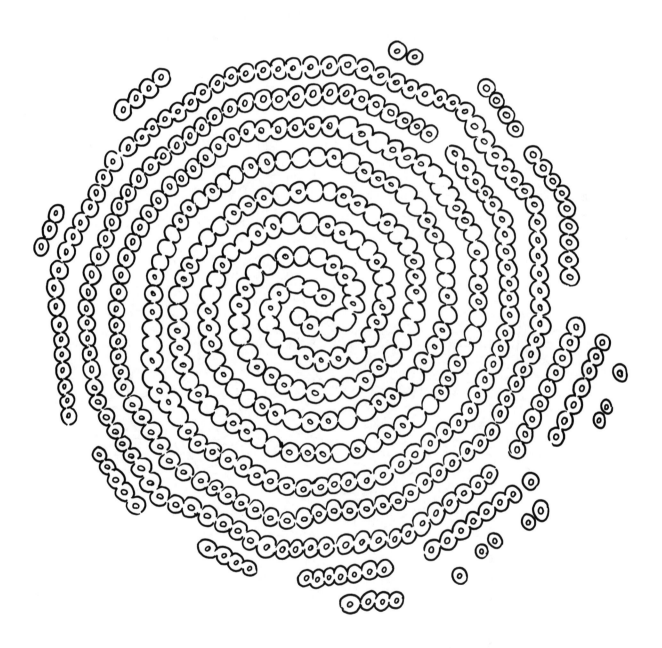

Internal Mandalas

We continue to encounter mandalas inside our bodies. Think, for example, of the cross-sections of all the different ducts inside the body, such as arteries, veins, and lymph ducts. They all display typical mandala shapes in cross section. The cross-section of a nerve also shows a mandala. The same is true of bone structures. The structure of the hepatic lobules, oriented towards the center of the central vein, also forms a natural mandala. The same goes for the cross-section of the intestinal tract.

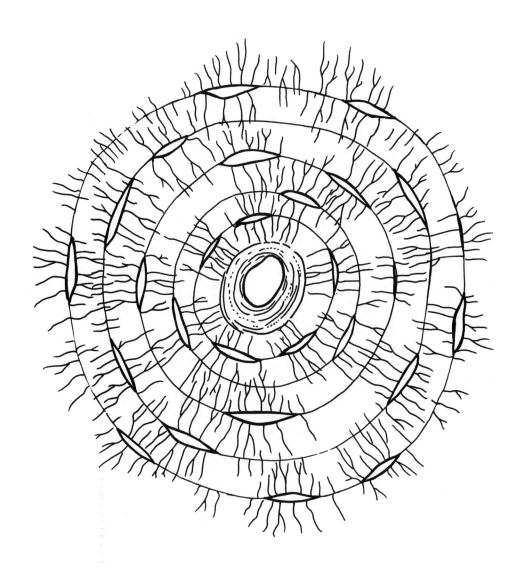

Deep in their anatomic structure, bones and their internal ducts reveal their mandala character.

External Mandalas

Leaving the inside of the body, we can see plenty of mandalas on the body's surface. Take, for instance, the spiral-shaped formations of our hair in some places. Similar spirals can be found on our skin, especially in fingerprints, which testify the uniqueness of a person. Fingerprints might soon replace our signatures because they are much more individual and cannot be forged.

Hair Mandala and Fingerprint Mandala

Human and Tree Mandalas

The close connection between humans and the rest of the world is revealed by the same mandala structure on the skin of old trees, whose bark is frequently covered in mandalas. Each wound that they have received in their lifetime through the loss of a branch also takes mandala shape. In fact, when we explore the world of trees more closely, we will find a great wealth of mandalas. Even more obvious in their mandala shape are the year rings of a tree. They keep a detailed record of the rich and poor years of a tree.

Nowadays, we can make diagnoses about a person's state of health by looking at a single hair in the same way that we look at the cross-section of a tree. Similar to a tree's year rings **(Fig. 1)**, the mandala layers in the cross-section of a hair **(Fig. 2)** can show how the person lived. Finally, the spine should be mentioned in this context as a person's main axis (similar to the earth's axis). It is represented here by a cross-section of an intervertebral disk **(Fig. 3)**.

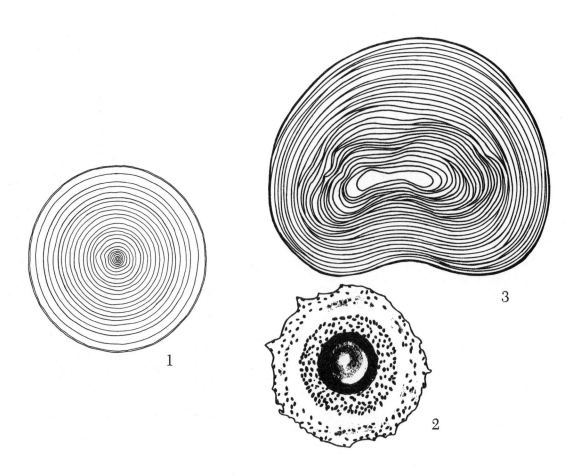

1

2

3

Leaf Mandalas

The most obvious mandalas in green trees are their leaves. A tree, if you place it upside down, can even represent our lungs. There is a strong trunk, which is the windpipe; two main branches leading to the lungs; and there are a large number of branches inside each lung. The pulmonary alveoli lining the branches of the lung-tree have the same function as the green leaves of a tree. Both lungs and trees exchange oxygen and carbon dioxide. The lung mandalas release oxygen from the air into the bloodstream and expel carbon dioxide from the bloodstream into the air. The leaf mandalas release oxygen into the surrounding air and absorb carbon dioxide from it. From this point of view, our breathing goes in circles from our internal tree to the external ones—like every circle, this too is a mandala.

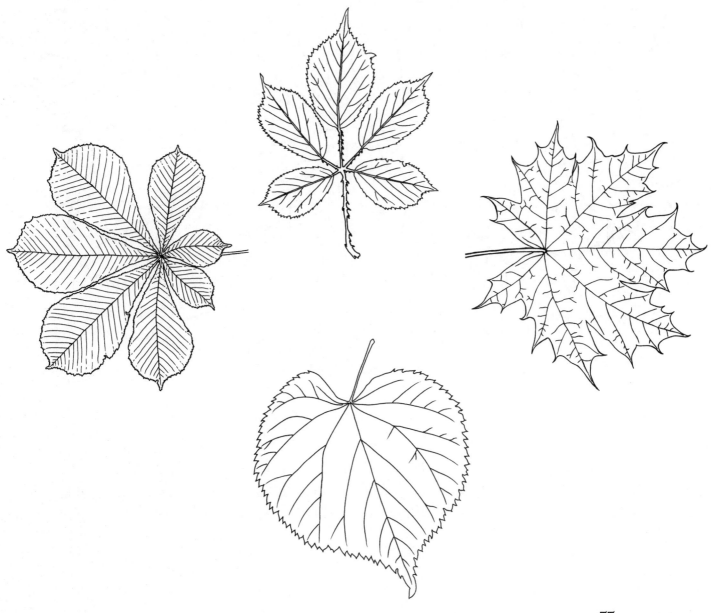

Every night, the leaves of the Lady's Mantle produce their own mandalas in the shape of a drop of water. Alchemists thought this drop of water was particularly suited for their work, and the Lady's Mantle Latin name, Alchemilla, still bears witness to this fact.

Fruit Mandalas

The fruits of a tree that develop from mandala-shaped flowers usually become mandalas as well, just as the fruits of mammals—the ova—are initially always mandalas. Even fruits such as pears or bananas, which as a whole are not mandala-shaped, always reveal their mandala character in cross–section.

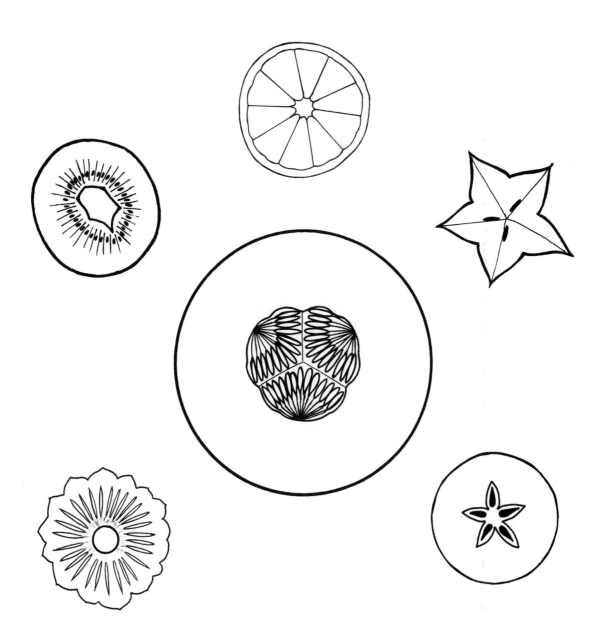

Back to Creation

In a person's outward appearance, the most dominant mandala is his or her head—even though it is not a perfect sphere. Even if we made the nose its center, the resulting picture would still not be symmetrical. Frequently, however, we can find near-perfect mandalas in the semi-spherical shapes of the female breasts. Their shape, which embodies all that is female, makes them wonderful representations of the moon and the Venus principle. We can see how important their mandala shape is as more and more women in western societies undergo cosmetic surgery to turn them into perfect mandalas. Externally, the surgery results in near-perfect spheres. However, they lose their natural softness and no longer follow gravity, whether a woman is standing up or lying down. Their moon characteristics are certainly not improved by the surgery, and it is doubtful whether their Venus characteristics are enhanced. Some women and their partners find these artificial products less enjoyable later on—which goes to show that we may be able to enhance nature's appearance, but not really nature itself. Our desire for perfect-looking mandalas shows us the other side of the coin: namely that, even where mandalas are concerned, we are not above putting shape before contents.

In the early years of life, the buttocks also come quite close to the mandala ideal; but during the course of life, they surrender to gravity and lose their mandala shape, to our great chagrin. We would much prefer two firm spheres that appeal to the mandala archetype within us. Even here, we help nature along with underwear with the necessary padding, just as certain brassières show off two perfectly shaped, spherical mandalas.

External Human Mandalas

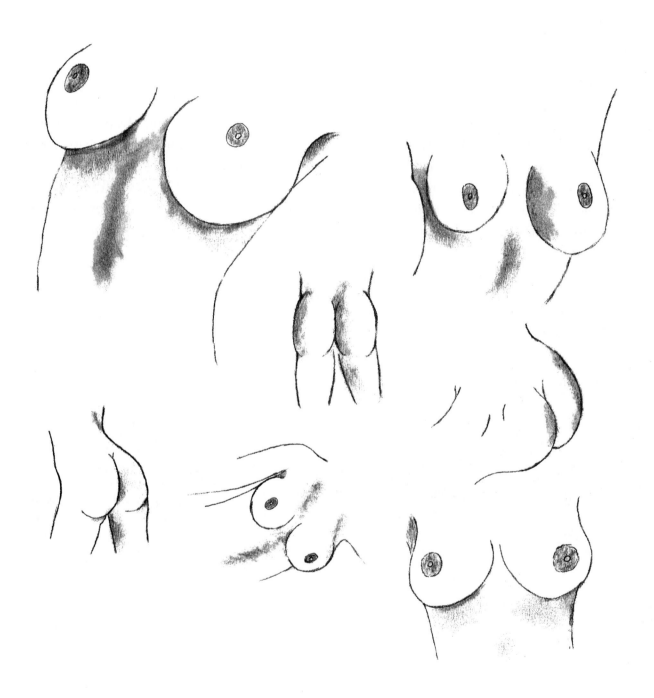

Eye Mandalas

One very obvious set of mandalas is located right on our faces: eye mandalas. They make a part of our brains visible because that is exactly what the eyeballs are: a little bit of our brains protruding to the outside. The iris and the pupil are further evidence of the principle of the mandala and draw our attention to the secret of the middle. The real middle is not the colored iris, also a mandala and full of secrets, but the pupil. It is like a black hole, all light disappears into it. The mandala-shaped retina is deep inside the pupil. The rod cells and retinal cones, also mandala-shaped, transform light impulses into electrical impulses. But the real secret takes us even further to the inside, as the electrical impulses are conducted along the optical nerve (in its cross-section a mandala) to the visual cortex of the brain.

Again, secret and solution can be found in the depths of the void, in absolute emptiness. The eyes of a loved one hold great fascination for lovers in all cultures, who must discover the secrets they hold.

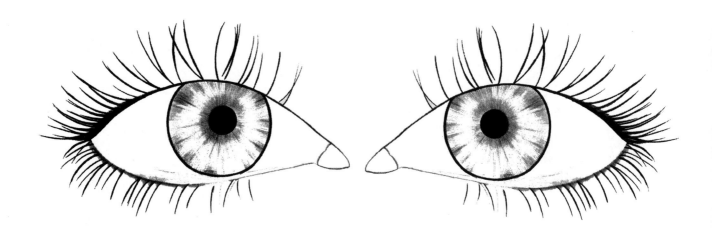

An Exercise for the Eye Mandalas

This exercise seems very simple, but it will enable you to delve very deeply into the secret of the middle and of the mandala. At the center of the mandala, the rules are different from those in the outside world of contrasts. People from eastern cultures assume that reality only exists outside polarity. In the world we think of as normal, two great swindlers—space and time—are at work, casting their web over us. At the center of the mandala, we have one of the mysterious meeting points of the two worlds, the real world of unity and the outside world of polarity. If you are able to give yourself over completely to the center of the mandala, you will be able, for a brief moment, to escape the limitations of space and time and immerse yourself in the timeless moment of the here and now. This is the goal of practically all meditation exercises.

Going by our experiences, these exercises are much more successful with mandalas that are alive. If you look into the eye of another person, you become immersed in one of the liveliest mandalas there is. But beware—don't underestimate this exercise, and follow the instructions very carefully.

At the center of the mandala, where time and space cease to exist—or rather, where they merge—you can see through all space and time. If you look your partner in the eye without blinking, you may experience very soon how his face changes; you can see younger and older images of his face shining through. After a while, you may even be able to recognize lighter and darker aspects to his personality. Initially, this may be very unfamiliar and even somewhat frightening. However, you are not meant to judge what you see. In fact, you cannot really be certain at any given moment whether it is a window to your partner's soul or your own reflection that you see. This is not really important anyway. First and foremost, we are trying to use our experiences to come closer to the secret of the mandala and the special quality of its center.

Until you know the area of transition between polarity and transcendence of time and space really well, you should not allow this exercise to last longer than ten minutes. Also, in the beginning, you should only practice with one partner. Afterwards, you will have to do some careful orientation exercises in order to return safely to the world of polarity.

A simple ear massage is best suited for this purpose. Start kneading your ear lobes with the thumbs and forefingers with both of your hands until they feel warm and alive. Continue your massage upward along the outer edge of the ear. Finally, use your forefingers to massage the crevices and indentations on the inside. You will have treated your whole body to a massage because the ear contains reflex zones for all the areas and organs of the body.

Once you have inwardly prepared for the adventure of journeying into the center and have found a suitable partner—who should be just as prepared as you are, since he or she will undergo similar experiences to your own—you can begin. Sit opposite each other on chairs so that your knees touch the edge of your partner's chair and so that you and your partner's knees are lined up alternately. Now straighten your upper body and briefly point with your finger to your left eye. Your partner should hold his or her gaze gently to this eye without blinking, without any comments and—most importantly—without looking away. All attention should be focused on the void, the black hole of the pupil. Soon, everything that surrounds it will become blurry because it is insignificant. The point is not simply to stare, but to gaze softly. You do not need to discover anything; you can simply wait for what the center of the mandala will reveal to you.

Do not worry if you shed a few tears; it is normal since you are trying so hard not to blink. Tears are also mandalas, and very useful ones at that. Many people, especially men, do not cry often enough; but now is a good opportunity. There is nothing odd about crying every now and then; actually, the person who never cries is really a bit strange. Why else would we have tear glands, if not to use them occasionally to relieve emotional pressure? Symbolically, tears represent pearls.

If you suddenly have to laugh and consequently ruin your concentration, then this is almost certainly a defense mechanism triggered by the fear of leaving the familiar world of polarity, where you are firmly in control. However, tears of laughter are still mandalas.

The Iris-Mandala: A Map of the Body and Soul

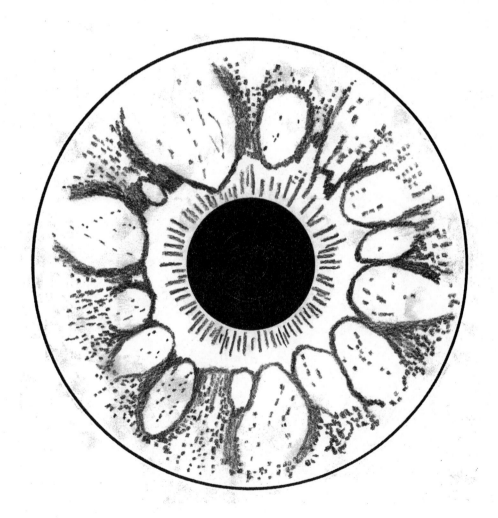

Taking the Eye Exercise a Bit Further

If you have enjoyed this simple exercise, it may be worth your while to extend it and explore it further. For instance, you could choose a living flower and gaze at the blossom mandala in meditation. You will experience once again that your eyes are much more than just a camera. Not only are they able to see what is inside and to have visions, but they can also see through the normal limitations of our reality.

In time you may be able to see the essence of the flower, if you can bring your gaze softly to the center of the blossom mandala. Again, the center makes these mysterious experiences possible, since the secret of the chosen flower lies at its center. Very sensitive people are actually able to empathize with the nature of Bach flowers and are directly touched by them similar to what Edward Bach must have experienced himself.

Eye Mandalas in Microcosm and Macrocosm

The eye can also show us an astonishing connection between microcosm and macrocosm. When we talk about the "eye of a hurricane," we are of course referring to the center of the storm.

Here, at the center, there is calm, just as in the nucleus of an atom or a cell. Although all power gathers in the center of the cyclone, no wind can be felt. Everything revolves around this center, yet we don't see or feel anything. The mandala with its mysterious

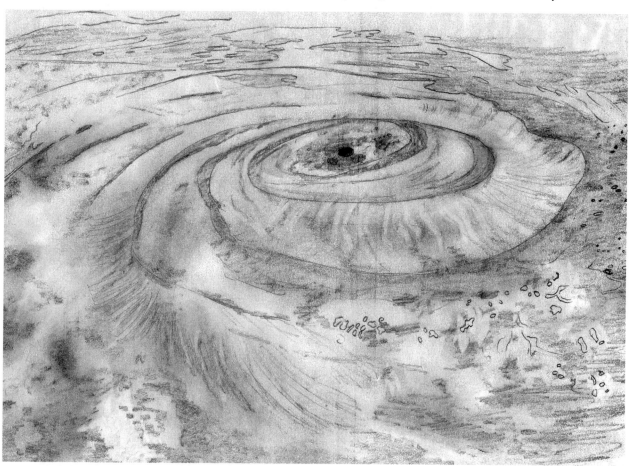

center comes into play again, as it has frequently done before—recall the case of the water whirlpool. If you have ever experienced the calm at the center of a great storm, you will have a feeling for the secret of its power, but no explanation.

Expanding on the Eye Mandala Exercise

If you have truly given yourself over to the mandalas at the center of a blossom and of your partner's eye, and you are certain that you can handle the forces at work there, it is possible to go one step further. You can actually look into your own personality and gain insight to those character traits with which you are not so familiar. This exercise must be done very carefully and should not be taken too far because there is no longer the opportunity to project unpleasant characteristics onto your partner. As you encounter your younger or older faces, you will probably find this quite an exciting experience. The realization that the past and future reside within us always, side by side, can help us to put things in order, and then let go.

When we encounter our bright sides with all their heavenly possibilities, we will be happy and even restored. However, if we come face to face with our shadows, it can be quite a shock. In this case, we recommend interrupting the exercise, especially if it has given rise to fear, and seeking the help of a therapist if you want to confront your darker side at a later stage. Of course, it would be sufficient simply to avoid this and similar exercises, but this is not a real solution to developing our awareness, as is required of us on our path through life. All major religions and traditions teach this. Christ asked us to "love our enemies." Our hidden darker sides are our most important and our most dangerous enemies. External enemies only become enemies because they remind us of the dark sides that are hidden in our own subconscious. But if we are at peace with our own shadows (our darker aspects), then all other enemies will cease to exist.

The Chakras

Eastern cultures recognize not only physical organs, but also energy organs: chakras. There are five chakras along the spinal column: (1) the root chakra, Muladhara, is at the pelvic floor; (2) the navel chakra is near the solar plexus; (3) Anahata, the heart chakra, is in the middle; (4) the larynx chakra, or the "Third Eye," Ajna, is above the heart chakra; and (5) Sahasrara-Padma is the uppermost chakra, situated just above the top of the head. Sensitive people can feel their energies and can sometimes even see them. They usually appear as colorful, spinning energy wheels. Most people can at least feel some radiation of heat if they hold an outstretched hand directly above the top of the head.

You can develop a deeper connection with your energy centers simply by coloring the chakras in the direction of energy flow, i.e., from bottom to top. Perhaps you would even like to try and color them in the "correct" colors as stipulated by the Rishis, who were seers in ancient India. You will find the colors indicated in the small print below each chakra. Maybe you will even feel yourself making a connection with the respective region while you are coloring.

The Sixth Chakra: Ajna, The Third Eye

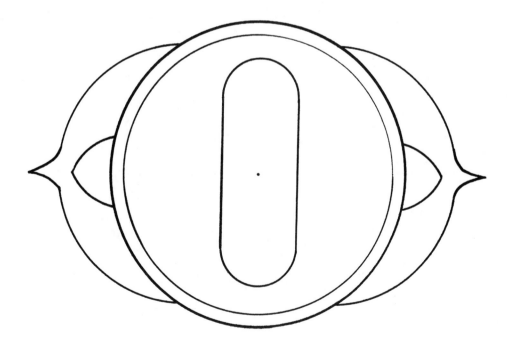

Coloring instructions: pale blue for the lingam at the center and the two lotus petals, white for the round area in the middle

The Remaining Chakras from Bottom to Top
The Root Chakra: Muladhara

Coloring instructions: yellow for all squares, red for all petals

The Second Chakra: Swadhisthana

Coloring instructions: white for the center, pale blue for the moon crescent, and red for the petals

The Third Chakra: Manipura, the Solar Plexus

Coloring instructions: red for the triangle, white for the circle, and blue for the petals

Exercise for the Fourth Chakra: Anahata, The Heart Chakra

PART 1:

While you are getting ready to meditate, imagine before your inner eye a loved one sitting in front of you. Look directly at his or her heart chakra, Anahata, and visualize the energy wheel with its warm shades of red. It may even start to spin in your imagination. At the same time, imagine the same chakra in the center of your own chest. In your imagination, allow your energy wheel to be aware of the corresponding energy wheel in your partner.

In time you will experience a band of energy forming between the two of you. When this happens, take as much time as you want to enjoy the flow of energy.

PART 2:

Repeat the exercise above, but instead of a loved person, imagine somebody whom you dislike intensely. Form the same heart-to-heart connection with this person. Perhaps you will experience what stands between you on this level. You may even be surprised to realize that your problem barely exists, or doesn't exist at all.

The Fourth Chakra: Anahata, The Heart Chakra and Energy Center

Coloring instructions: warm green for the hexagram, white for the circle, and red for the petals

The Fifth Chakra: Vishuddha, the Larynx

Coloring instructions: white for the center, silver for the half-moon crescent, and purple for the petals

The Seventh Chakra: Sahasrara-Padma, the Crown Chakra

Coloring instructions: white for the center circle, and all the colors of the rainbow for the petals

The Crown Mandala in Various Cultures

The crown chakra is also called lotus. Both terms emphasize the mandala character. If the top chakra is open, Christian tradition talks of a halo. The crown, which adorns royal heads to this day, is but a pale reflection of a halo. Over time, as royalty became less significant, crowns became more and more elaborate. They were always made from gold, the metal of the sun principle, and were adorned with precious stones. Even though the crown—like the laurel wreath—is a mandala and most precious stones are cut to mandala shape, the result, however shiny and sparkly, is rather modest in comparison to an opened seventh chakra.

With Buddha, the state of the opened crown chakra is often emphasized by the kundalini snake which rises up behind him and towers over his head with the majestic broad head of the king cobra. The snake's deliverance is also thus portrayed; it is no longer destined to creep around on its belly and eat dust (as ordained in the Bible), but stands tall and becomes the symbol of enlightenment and unity. Herein also lies the root of the Indian tradition of snake charming. The charmer with his flute celebrates a ritual, which should really take place inside him and all of us.

1 Further information on this exercise can be found in my first mandala book, Mandalas of the World.

Snake Mandala

In Christianity, the snake has been assigned a lowly place as an extension of the devil, but in many other traditions, it has achieved varying degrees of deliverance. Take, for example, the uroboros symbol of the snake biting its own tail, which comes from the Aborigines in Australia. This mandala shape shows that the beginning and the end are one and that a perfectly fulfilled life does not know a beginning or an end.

In Western esoteric teaching, the Hermes staff is a symbol that is similar to the representations of Buddha with the kundalini snake. The symbol consists of two snakes that represent the energies of Ida and Pingala, which meet in the middle, the crown chakra, thus symbolizing fulfillment. The staff of Aesculapius, the international emblem of physicians, clearly shows the physician's mission to raise the snake, or rather to free lowly creatures and matter from their material aspects and elevate them.

The Mandala Snake of the Aborigines Guarding
its Mandala Eggs

Living in the Mandala

Humans are mandalas, since we originally used to live inside one. Even though humans have become more cultured and civilized through the course of evolution, we always have remained close to nature; even today, we are closer to nature than we would sometimes like to be. Like all creatures of nature, early humans looked for places to live within nature, and later, when we had the ability, we would still shape them with nature in mind. Most animals live in mandala-shaped dwellings—just think of birds' nests, worm and snake holes, the spherical hives of wasps, molehills, mouse holes, and caves. We simply cannot get past the mandala!

The Hexagram Mandala

The hexagram—two superimposed triangles, as in the Star of David—often symbolizes the connection between heaven and earth. The shape is very common in nature, as in the honeycomb in bees' nests. The picture below shows a typical example.

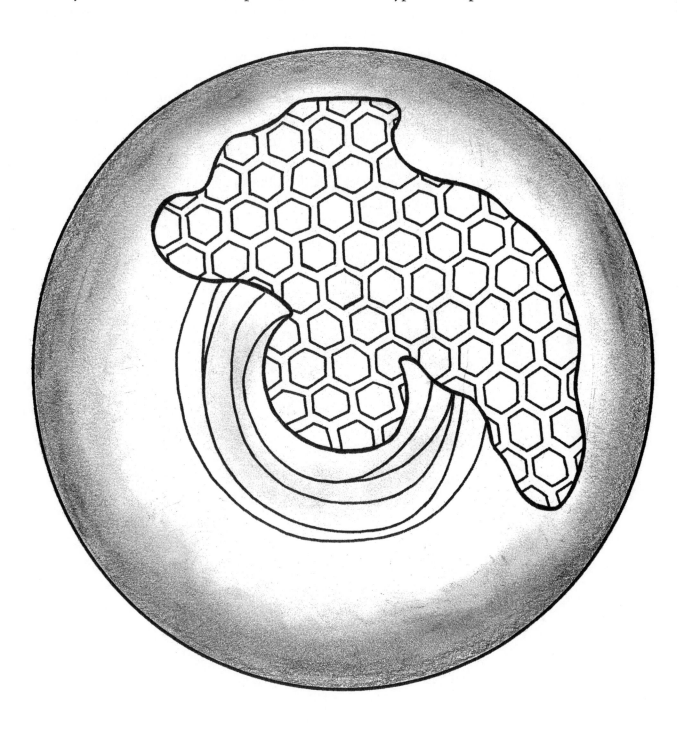

Moving from Mandala to Mandala

Just as the homes of animals, the earliest homes of humans were always mandalas, just as were the homes of the gods. But while animals and humans sought refuge in the many caves that Mother Nature offered, the gods chose the peaks of mountains, which then became holy. Whether it is the top of Mount Olympus, Mount Fuji, Mount Aranajula, or Mount Kailash, they are all mandalas when we look at them from above. Sometimes humans tried to be closer to their gods and found dwelling places in the mountain. They never settled at the very top, but rather somewhere around the midway point, as on Mount Athos and the Meteora monasteries in Greece, or the hermit dwellings called tigers' nests in Bhutan.

Without a doubt, man's first dwelling place is the ovum, a perfect mandala. After fertilization by the male semen, it becomes slightly eccentric for a while, but soon regenerates its stable mandala shape. Every subsequent division of cells briefly disturbs the mandala, but the perfect circle is assumed again very quickly in the shape of the morula.

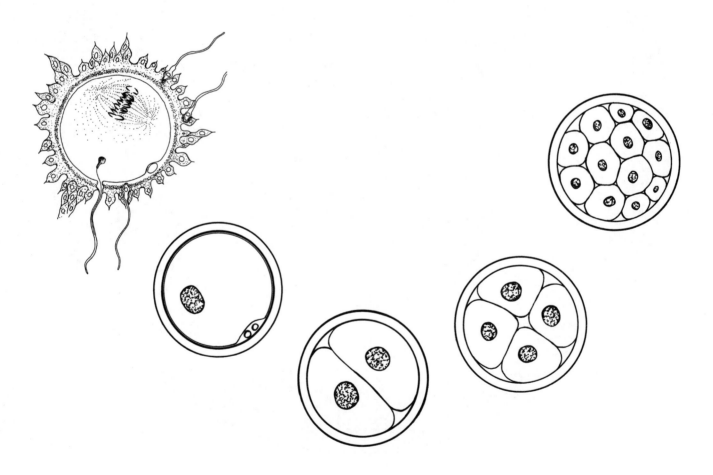

Growing Inside the Mandala

Once the morula develops to form the embryo, the mandala structure is maintained inside. The home of the growing embryo, the amniotic sac, is also a mandala, as is the uterus which surrounds it. What is more, the mother's stomach increasingly assumes the wonderful mandala shape.

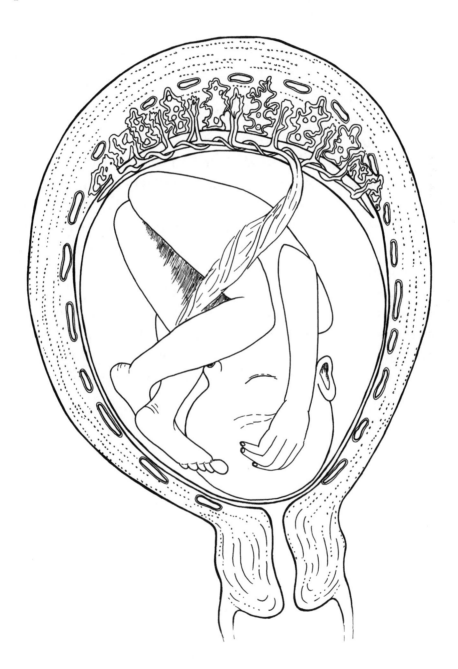

Why We Crave the Unity of the Beginning

As typical mammals, humans need cave-like homes, even after we have left the protective caves of our mothers' wombs. We would like to go back to that cave and let our loving parents do everything they can to provide an appropriate nest. Everything about this nest woul have to be round, in the figurative sense of the mandala. The best solution would be the external pouch of the kangaroo, which replaces the internal amniotic sac. People in archaic societies have quite successfully imitated the kangaroo by using lengths of fabric to carry their infants close to their bodies. In our industrialized society, many mothers today use similar devices to preserve their babies' sense of security as experienced in the cave of the womb. In other words, they are trying to maintain the round mandala atmosphere for a warm, secure start in life.

Unfortunately, there comes a point when humans have to leave the primordial mandala cave. But we will aim never to lose it, to be able to fall back on it for regeneration, and generally as the basis of our lives. Early man retreated to the caves that Mother Nature provided. They were naturally round, and early man would light campfires to keep the cave warm, as he was in the womb. Even today, the apartments and houses of many people resemble cozy caves. This is particularly evident in the bedroom, the room designed for regeneration, ensuring nightly regression.

In any case, the bed is a representation of the cave of the womb. Some people even make a mandala shape with their bodies when they curl up into a fetus position during sleep. People who need to feel especially safe and secure often require two bed covers: one to lie on and one to cover them to make a cave that is soft all over. Even though we are not always conscious of it, it is clear that we all return to the Great Mother during the night, looking for the security of unity in her cave.

Mandala Dwellings

The closer people remain to nature, and also to their own nature, the closer their dwelling places will be to the mandala. No sooner had they left their caves, than early humans tried to build spherical mandala-shaped caves outside. Often their quest for the mandala was made difficult through a lack of suitable materials. Thanks to their ideal building material, the Eskimos were at a great advantage, and their spherical igloos can be considered particularly successful attempts at the mandala shape. This is especially true when we consider that snow consists of mandala-shaped crystals and ultimately of solidified mandala water-drops. The typical mandala houses of an African kraal remain just as close to the original pattern as do the teepees of the Native American tribes.

From God's perspective, it is not easy to decide whether the above depicts a kraal, a circle of Native American teepees, or maybe early Germanic roundhouses.

Circle and Straight Line

In our modern society, we have given up the life in the mandala in many respects, even though we will never really manage to leave it behind. Nevertheless, the right angle and the straight line have become the rule in our everyday environment. In reality, however, there is no such thing as a straight line or a right angle, as both are based on a trick of the senses. If we look at the horizon, we can easily see that every straight line is in effect a circle, if we follow it long enough. If we fly a plane straight ahead, we will eventually circle the mandala Earth.

Therefore what we consider a straight line is always a trick or maybe even a flaw in our thinking; still, the straight line gains more and more power over our lives. The behavioral scientist, Konrad Lorenz, warned us about the consequences of these shoebox worlds that increasingly dominate our lives. We have replaced the rounded shapes of the cave with the right-angled world of our apartments and houses, in which we live increasingly apart and feel less safe and secure. In religious buildings, however, we still have the mandala shape—in outlines, ceiling constructions, floor mosaics, vaults and windows. We encounter them all over the world when we make our way from nature to culture. Whether we visit Chinese pagodas, Indian star cities, or the churches of Christianity, the circle of the mandala is everywhere.

Leisure-Time Mandalas

When there is no strict order in our lives, even in our free time, we still lean towards the mandala, just as in the early beginnings of humanity. Like animals that gather around a water hole, people of all kinds like to sit in a circle around a campfire. Our dining tables are still as round as that of King Arthur and his companions, unless—of course—they have been arranged for a business lunch or a meeting. Food is always served on mandala-shaped plates, and we drink out of glasses, goblets, cups, and jugs of the same shape. A very sophisticated cuisine, such as the French, always aims to arrange dishes as mandalas, and even the simple Italian pizza has a mandala shape.

If we want to celebrate a special occasion, we almost always choose a mandala: a cake. A birthday cake at a children's party is, and will always be, a shining mandala. Even candles, which we light for festive occasions, form mandalas, as do fireworks. If you think about it, every light in itself is a mandala: light bulbs, most lamps, and, especially electrical sparks, which—like small explosions—burst forth into space.

Pizza: A Symbolic Piece of Art

Everyday Life with Mandalas

Our everyday lives are filled with mandalas, even though we do not always consciously notice. The drain and stopper in the kitchen sink and bathtub are mandalas. The water drains from the bath in a mandala whirlpool, and bubbles form mandalas in boiling water. Each pot is a mandala, old and new water faucets, and all the buttons that we push and turn daily in our cars and on our stereos.

So whenever we turn a knob, we turn a mandala. When we drive a car, we hold onto a mandala with our hands and move along the street on four tire mandalas. Our trains roll on many mandalas. Even airplanes roll along on mandalas before they leave the earth, but once in the air, they rely on mandalas too. Propellers are simply fast-spinning mandalas, and so are the turbines of a jet engine. And finally, if we daydream about life beyond our planet, the UFOs that we picture usually have a mandala shape.

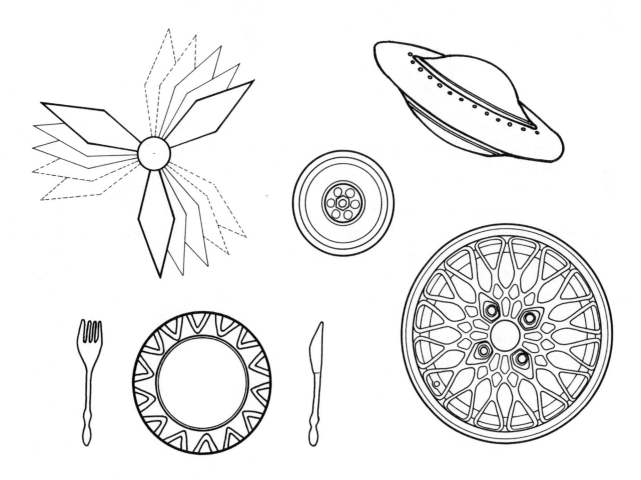

Precious Mandalas

Even the technical world of our everyday lives cannot cope without mandalas. I am not just talking about the wheels of industry in a figurative sense (the history of human progress is ultimately based on the wheel, which is a mandala).

If all mandalas stopped spinning, all wheels would stand still and our modern world would soon perish. We could simply not exist without mandalas, but do we ever really think about this fact?

In highly developed countries, high self-esteem is based almost exclusively on technological and economic sophistication. The economic aspect—for most materialists the be-all and end-all—has been captured in the mandala right from the beginning. The economy of practically all countries in the world has always been ruled by coins, and all coins are mandala-shaped. Originally they were mainly made of gold, which represents the sun principle and unity. The first gold coins were used in cults and they symbolized the perfection of god and his creation. Even though we have more modern means of payment today, coins still play a central role. Again, we have discovered the mandala and its magic right at the beginning of human progress.

Old and New Coins

The Path as a Mandala

Wherever we go, we will never be without the basic pattern of the mandala. With that in mind, it is not surprising that the mandala is the best way to represent our path through life. Practically all legends of creation have chosen—consciously or subconsciously—the mandala as the representation of the path. The modern theory of the Big Bang is no exception. Suddenly, and nobody knows why, there was this big bang. From that point on, everything moved away from the center of the explosion at rapid speed. Astrophysicists have proven that all celestial bodies in this universe are moving away from each other. You may want to picture this like a balloon: as you blow it up, all points on its surface move away from the center and from each other at the same time.

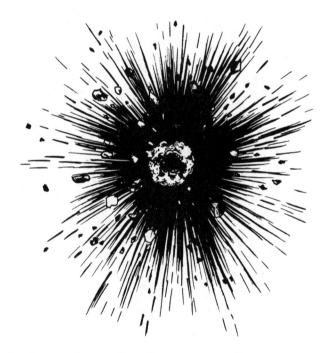

Sometime in the distant future this phenomenon of expansion is expected to reverse, so that creation will return to its point of origin. At least this is what scientists such as Stephen Hawking believe. This takes us to the old Indian myth of creation, which says that Brahma's taking a breath brought forth our creation. At the moment we are in the exhaling phase; the subsequent inhaling will bring an end to this world and time (yuga). In general, the mythologies of all the different cultures use very similar images to describe the phenomenon. Creation is a mandala process, which—like all living things—follows its own rhythm.

Myths of Creation in Different Cultures

From the early days of human history to the religious myths of the major religions today, creation is usually represented in a mandala. Below is an example of the Navajo myth, shown in three sand mandalas. According to these depictions, everything is created from a holy place in the center, from which the four main crops emerge to grow between the four holy mountains. The circular shape of the rainbow queen, who holds all of creation together, surrounds them. All three are open to the east, towards the light.

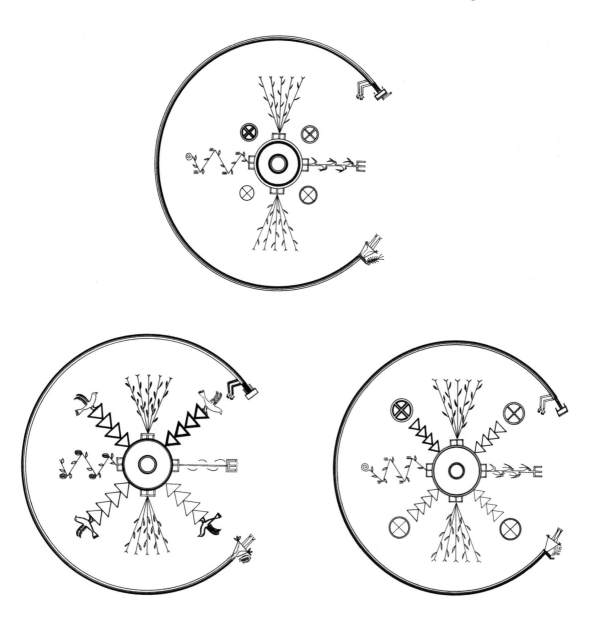

Mandala Myths

If we look closely at the Christian myths, we will notice that they are just as firmly rooted as those of science. In paradise, the androgynous Adam, who had been formed from red earth, took a few steps out into polarity. First he lost one side, or—thanks to Luther's poetic license—one rib to Eve; then they both ate from the tree of polarity, whose fruit bore the knowledge of good and evil. Together, they were expelled from the world of unity, which did not yet know any opposite or any judgment of good and evil. In the world outside, they had the express task from God to go out and rule the world, and one day return to unity.

Whether ruling the world meant enslaving it and inflicting its present state on it is doubtful. After all, it could have meant that they were to rise above polarity and regain unity on a higher level. The New Testament says quite clearly that if we do not turn around and become like children again, then we will never reach the kingdom of God. In the context of the mandala, this can only mean that we should walk the entire path, right to the edge, and then turn around and rediscover unity, or paradise—the Garden of Eden or the kingdom of God within ourselves, at the center.

If we consider that the Bible also points out that we have the kingdom of God inside us, it becomes clear that even our holy scripture is much closer to the knowledge of the mandala than we might think. From that point of view, there is not much reason to seek refuge in the Veda or the sutras of Buddhism.

The gods of antiquity, who have provided a lot of material for our myths, are also connected to the mandala via the planets.

Saturn: Guardian of the Threshold and its Mandala Moons

Our Moon: Source of Many Myths

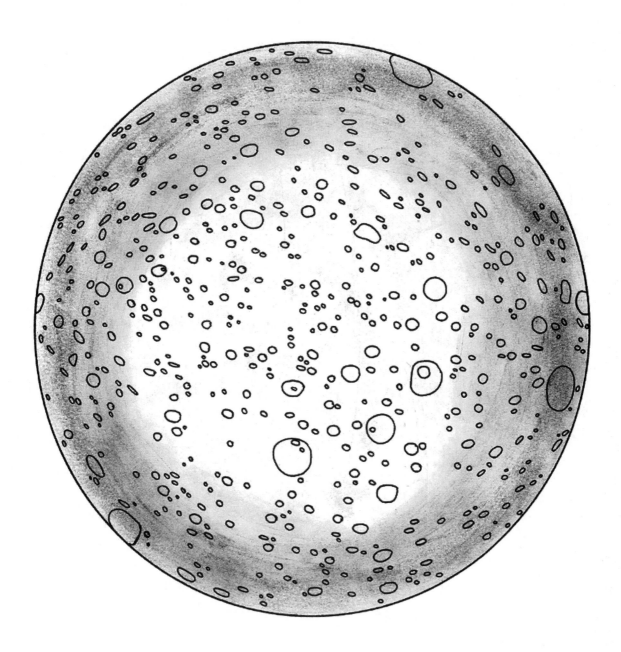

The moon, like all celestial bodies, is a mandala, and its surface is marked by the mandala shapes of meteorites that hit it.

The Creation from a Hermetic Point of View

The following mandalas show an attempt by the English hermetic Robert Fludd to merge the Judeo-Christian myth of creation with the Gnostic view of Hermes Trismegistus. The first mandala depicts chaos: the earth comes into being during the seemingly unordered struggle between hot and cold, wet and dry.

The Vision of the Cosmos

The second mandala reveals the beginning of the cosmos, which establishes an identity between the absolute and the individual.

The First Created Light Enters the World

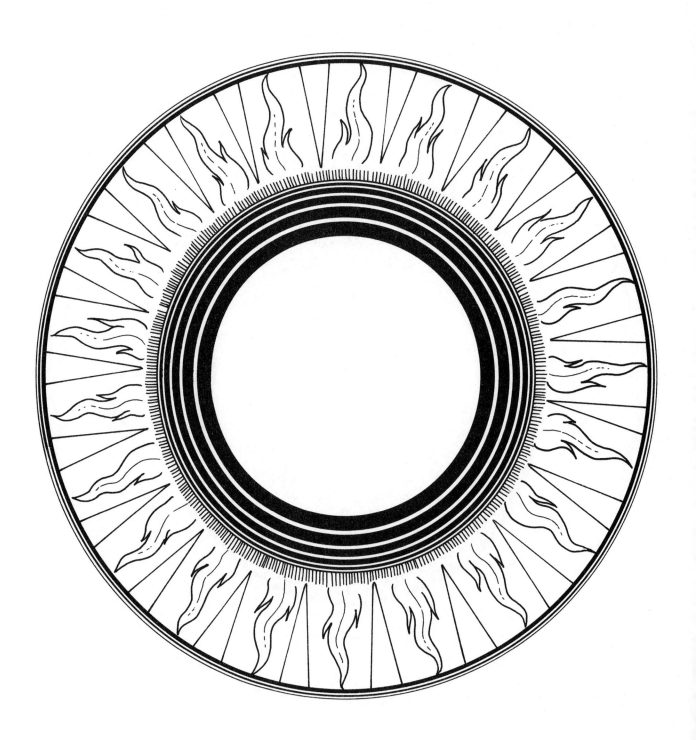

The Four Elements Are Created

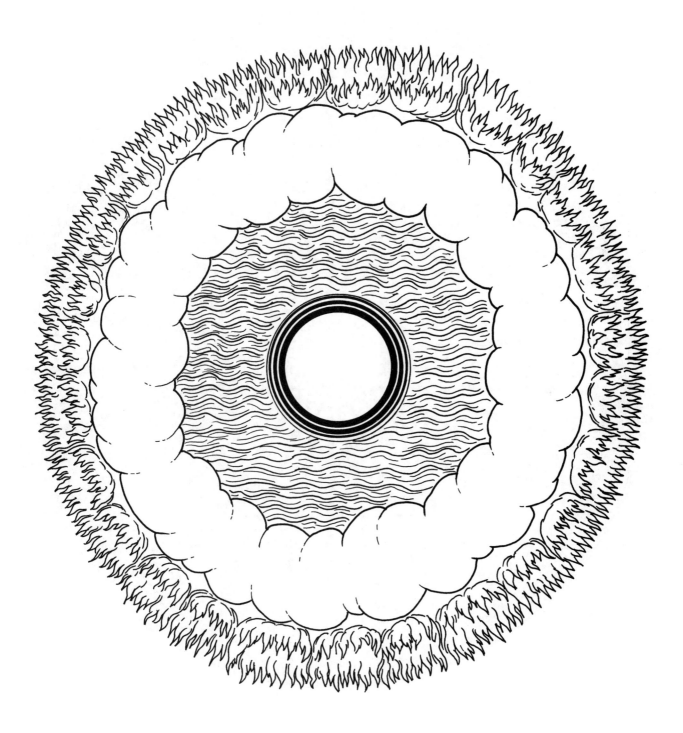

Mandala: Many Paths, One Goal

The Shell of a Radiolarian

The Center of the Mandala: the Same Goal for Everybody

If we let this last natural mandala take its effect on us, we may be able to see why all holy scriptures have chosen this pattern to describe the path through life. Eastern teachings make it clear that all paths lead back to the same center. If we take the center to mean unity, then there can be only one center and one unity, an opposite pole to polarity, in a manner of speaking. Even mathematics today does not doubt that this is true and that the center and its midpoint are not of this world. Mathematics assumes that a point is one-dimensional and therefore does not belong to this polar world, in which everything needs at least two sides to exist, and three dimensions to establish itself in space.

We should really reconsider our conviction that only we know the way. There is, for example, the eastern view that many paths lead to the same goal. Indian mandalas almost always have four gates, a sign that we can find unity at the center from all four points of the compass. Christianity and Islam, the two main religions that emerged from Judaism, have far too often in their histories disrespected other religions by maintaining that they alone knew the right way. This led to a great deal of fanaticism and many wars, and in no way does it do justice to the mandala. If Christians stride bravely on their path to find enlightenment, or God's kingdom (inside themselves), then they will not mind if a few Buddhists and Hindus arrive there ahead of them.

The World of the Paths

Islamic Mandala Depicting the Path Through Life

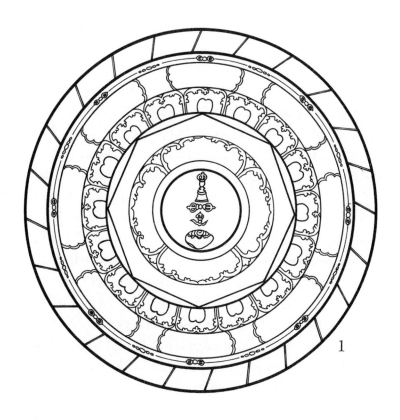

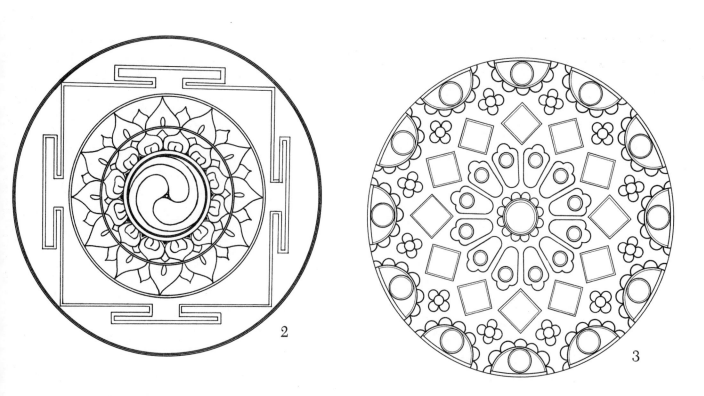

1. Buddhist Mandala, 2. Hindi Mandala, 3. Christian Mandala

The Mandala and the Seasons of Life

We can find everything in the mandala. We can find each transition in life in it. We can color a mandala for each stage of life, childhood, youth, midlife, and old age. In my book *Mandalas of the World*, there is even an old mandala of the dead.

In these mandalas, we can recognize the four seasons of life that are also the four seasons of the year. (Coincidentally, a day and a year are both mandalas.) The mandala can enlighten us about a few misconceptions, for example that the midpoint in life is something to be depressed about. The mandala shows quite clearly that, on the contrary, it is the high point of life: we have now reached the periphery of the mandala, where the tension is greatest. From here, we can now make it easier for ourselves and let our souls start on the way home, eventually ending at the center of the mandala, the place of deliverance and death. But here is where our problem lies. Since we view death not as deliverance but as an end and something extremely frightening, most of us do not want to turn back; we cling to the periphery of the mandala, at the greatest distance from the center. Consequently, many people consider the midpoint in life a low instead of a high point. The mandala might be able to put us back on the right track.

The Native American Mandala of the Four Life Seasons

The Midpoint in Life: the Edge of the Mandala

The Bible's request to turn around and become like children again is greatly reinforced by talking about the midpoint in life. We either turn around of our own free will, or face increasing catastrophe ("turning back" in Greek is *he katastrophe*). The real task for the soul consists in confronting the opposite pole of one's soul and to free it, according to C.G. Jung. He theorized that a woman has to realize her *animus*, the male part of her soul, and a man his *anima*, the female aspect of his soul. If we do not, we will suffer.

Who Am I Within the Mandala?

Close your eyes for a moment and focus on your center. Sink deep into meditation and ask yourself: do you live up to your sex? Has your life been influenced by experiences and shapes which do it justice? Or have you ended up in the patterns of your opposite pole? Open your eyes again and now color in the mandala from the center, drawing the shapes that have influenced you so far.

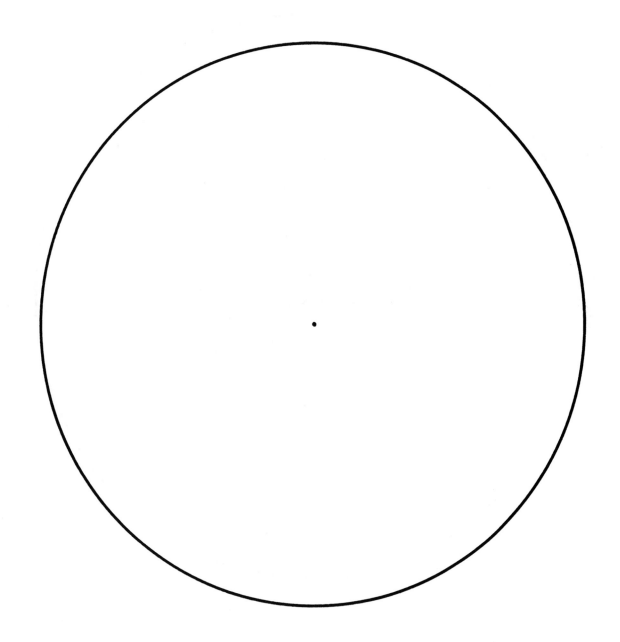

Anima Mandala

Color the center of the following incomplete mandala with soft, feminine colors and complete the missing structures.

Animus Mandala

Now color the center of the following incomplete mandala with strong, masculine colors and complete the missing structures.

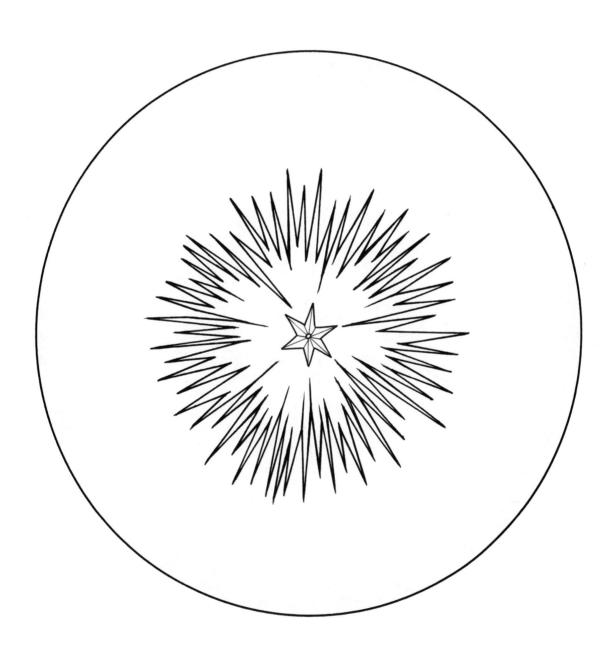

Spring and Summer

Color this mandala, starting from the center. Express your journey from birth to the midpoint in life, or in other words, from spring to summer.

Fall and Winter

Now color this mandala from the outside toward the center. Try to express your return journey from the midpoint all the way to deliverance, through fall and winter, so to speak.

Cultural Mandalas

The same phenomenon that we have encountered in nature will follow us in the wide realm of cultures. Once we have trained our eyes to see mandalas, we will see them everywhere. To my knowledge, there is not one culture that did not know the meaning of mandalas and did not manifest them in their places of religious worship. Ancient stone circles are witness to this fact, the most famous among them being Stonehenge in England. We do not know that much about these megalithic structures: we are not sure how old they are, what purpose they served, nor even how early man was able to build them. Even today, we would have great trouble building something similar. But one thing we know is certain: almost all of these structures have a mandala shape. People who regard this marvel as a mere coincidence are definitely not realists.

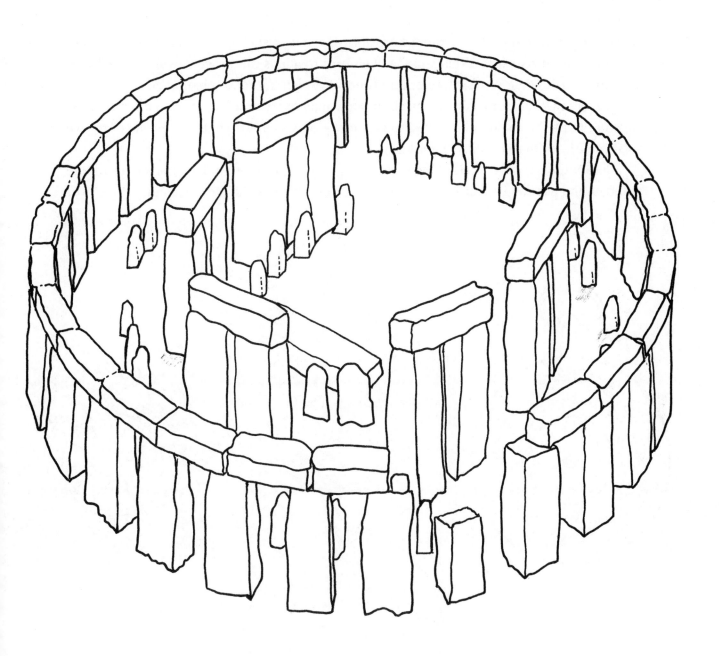

Stonehenge

The Mandala Calendar

Some of the circular images below are types of calendars, at least in some respect. For example, they may have been tools used to determine the day of spring equinox. Again, we are not sure how our early ancestors were able to arrive at such exact results regarding the calendar. Authors such as Erich von Daniken turn to aliens for answers, which is really no more outlandish than some of the other efforts at explaining these phenomena.

In any case, all our calendars are ultimately mandalas, from the tried and tested solar calendar to the lunar calendar. A year always completes a circle, whether it is one of twelve solar months or thirteen lunar months.

Everything related to the calendar and to time turns around in the circle of the mandala and has done so since time immemorial, as shown by the Aztec calendar stone over the page.

Time in the Mandala

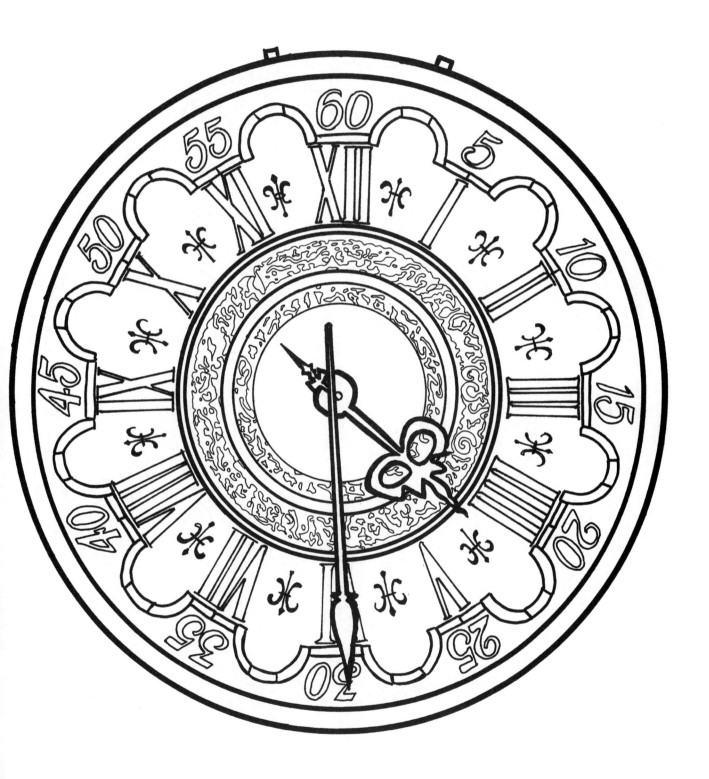

Aztec Calendar Stone

Life Mandalas

From the point of view of spiritual philosophy, the most important calendar in life is probably the horoscope with its ancient principles and patterns. It is the real mandala of life. In it we find an underlying timetable for life, a mosaic of little pieces, including the signs of the zodiac, planets, houses, and the relationships between them. All of these energies follow the system of the ancient principles or archetypes, which we have already encountered several times. Without them, we cannot really understand or explain anything. If you are not familiar with archetypes, it may be better for you to start with the ancient principle mandalas that come later in the book before working with the mandalas on the following pages. This may help you develop a basic understanding of these principles so that you can really enjoy coloring the ancient principle "gateau" that follows.

If you have an understanding of these archetypes and you know your own ancient principle pattern, you may find it a positive challenge to color the painting of your own life on the next page.

Occidental Zodiac

Chinese Zodiac

The Northern Hemisphere and its Signs of the Zodiac

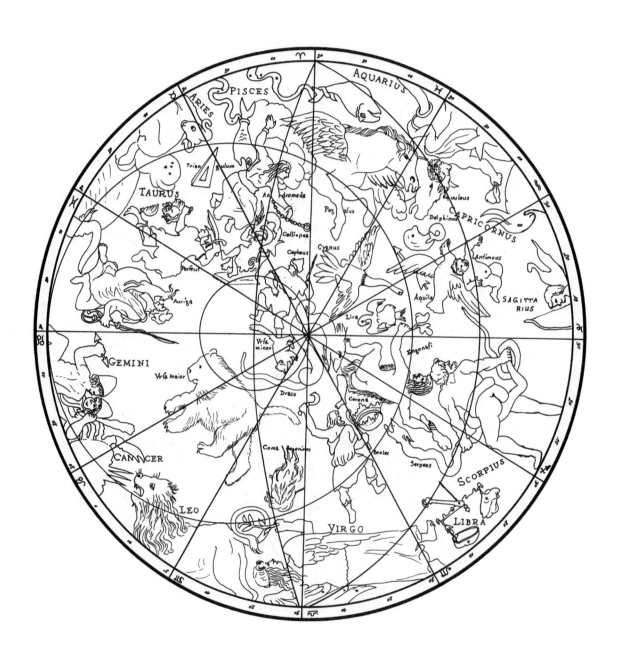

The Southern Hemisphere and its Signs of the Zodiac

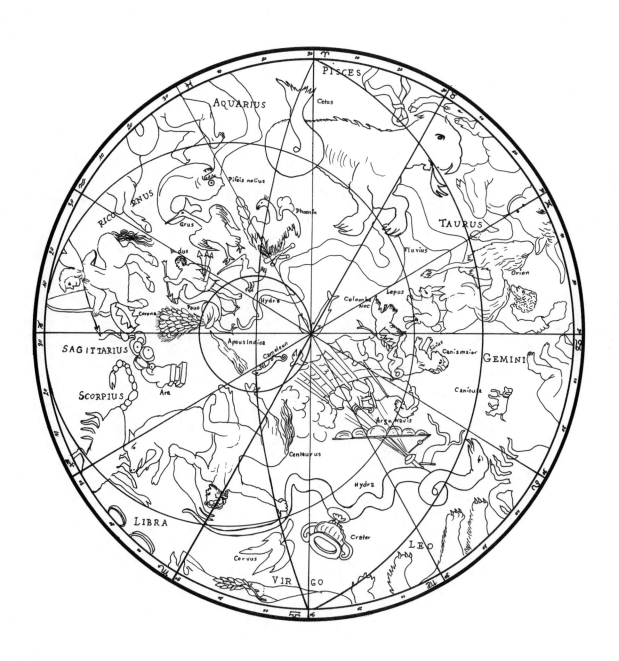

The Principle of the Beginning, Ascribed to the War God, Mars

"Nothing ventured, nothing gained."

Principle: the beginning, the initial spark, the first impulse and its implementation, the deed, enforcement, aggression, battle spirit, decision, and undirected energy that is quickly used up

Color: red

Quality: hot and dry

Shape: pointed, sharp

The Principle of Reconciliation Ascribed to Venus, the Goddess of Love

"I send out my warmth and find it again in others."
ANAIS NIN

Principle: balance, reconciliation, harmony, beauty, connection, ability to enjoy, sensuality, and love

Color: pink, pale blue, pastels

Quality: well tempered

Shape: well proportioned

The Principle of Receiving, Ascribed to the Moon Goddess

"You have to open your hands if you want to fetch water."
CHINESE PROVERB

Principle: feminine, passive, reflecting, flowing; cyclic, changing, the subconscious, and the soul

Color: white, silver, green

Quality: cool, damp

Shape: soft, flowing, enveloping

The Principle of Charisma, Ascribed to the Sun God

"God hides from man's spirit, but He reveals Himself to his heart."
TALMUD

Principle: creative, masculine, self-expression, self-confidence, vitality, strength, courage, and the center

Color: golden (yellow)

Quality: warm, dry

Shape: centered, radial, strong

The Principle of Expansion, Ascribed to Zeus (Jupiter), the Father of the Gods

"Man holds within him heaven and earth."
HILDEGARD VON BINGEN

Principle: growth, wealth, abundance, enrichment, expansion into space, generosity, fulfillment, finding of meaning, religion, and synthesis

Color: crimson, purple

Quality: warm, dry

Shape: massive, widely spreading, lush, baroque

The Principle of Concentration, Ascribed to Saturn

"Ultimately, we are all on our own. Each person needs to do the most important things by himself."

Principle: regularity, structure, concentration on the essential, maturing, responsibility, discipline, age, crystallization, condensing, conservation, and reduction

Color: black, midnight blue

Quality: cold, dry

Shape: clear, structured, hard

The Principle of Communication, Ascribed to Hermes (Mercury), the Gods' Messenger

"Who is wise? He who learns from all."
TALMUD

Principle: mediation, exchange, network, flexibility, neutrality, catalyst, breathing, language, and intellect

Color: bright yellow

Quality: cool, airy

Shape: linked, branching out, delicate

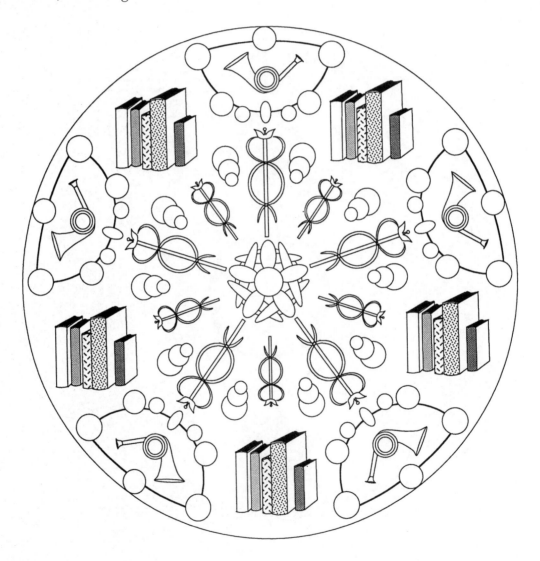

Following the seven classic principles, here are the three new planets and their ancient principles.

The Principle of Transcendence, Ascribed to Poseidon (Neptune), the Sea God

"If the windows of perception were clean, everything would appear to man the way it is: infinite."
WILLIAM BLAKE

Principle: solution and unification, resolving the superficial in order to throw light on the essential, deception, disappointment, illusion, and dream

Color: water-colored, iridescent

Quality: cool, damp

Shape: transparent, without limits, blurred

The Principle of Depolarization, Ascribed to Uranus, the God of Heaven

"You are free to do whatever you want, you only need to be prepared to bear the consequences."
SHELDON KOPP

Principle: liberation, breaking free of set structures, transgressing the norm, breaking out, departure, breakthrough, change, androgynous nature, and removed from the norm

Color: orange, garish colors

Quality: cool

Shape: bizarre, unusual, eccentric

The Principle of Die and Become, Ascribed to Hades (Pluto), the God of the Underworld

"So long as you don't have this, this 'Die and become!'
you are a sad guest on this dark earth."
GOETHE

Principle: metamorphosis (changing shape), metanoia (changing one's mind), turning back, remorse, development, polarization, self-control and compulsive behavior, sexuality, procreation, and the inner dragon fight

Color: contrasting combinations, such as black and white, black and red

Quality: hot and cold, damp

Shape: asymmetrical, extreme, ugly

Mandalas: Cultural Universality and Ecumenical Spirituality

The fact that all major religions recognize and respect the mandala shows the importance that all cultures and belief systems give to the path to one's own center. One could even regard the mandala as the path of the different religions. At the center—where the experience and realization of unity is still fresh and where religions are born—there are virtually no contradictions. Of course, this is to be expected. How could there be any contradictions within unity? But the further a given religion moves toward the periphery of the mandala and tries to find security in commandments and dogmas, the easier it is for conflicts to arise between the religions, or rather their official representatives. On the very edge of the periphery, where tension is greatest, different religious groups seem to have irreconcilable differences and are sometimes even willing to go to war. At the center, where there is unity, this would be unthinkable. Religions have to walk the entire path—much like people, it seems—but along the way, they can take care of their roots, their connection with the center.

Teachers of religious education who guide their students towards experiencing the center of the mandala are actively watering the roots of their religion. It is ironical and typical of our time that they are often not very popular with those who follow different ideas on the periphery of the mandala. I have experienced myself the extent of openness in our day and age; people are searching everywhere inside and outside of the established religions. My first Zen experiences were with Jesuits; there are many Christian monasteries today where monks teach contemplation and meditation. In eastern monasteries and ashrams, I have found that Christians are gladly accepted and given shelter on their way, without ever becoming the victim of any missionary attempts.

A Mandala Journey from Religion to Religion

The mandala has always been viewed as a spinning wheel. It was not just Christianity that used this motif in the window rosettes of the Romantic Age or the natives of North America who lived with the medicine wheel. Human life begins and ends in a spiral current through which the soul is sucked into the body and from which it eventually frees itself again. This current, which everyone has experienced and can experience again with the help of reincarnation therapy, is probably the primal pattern of a spinning wheel. Taoism explains the secret of the mandala wheel in a particularly nice way in the following verse:

> *"The spokes form the wheel,*
> *Where they are not, there lies meaning.*
> *The clay forms the jug,*
> *Where it is not, there lies its meaning.*
> *The walls form the room,*
> *Where they are not, there lies their meaning.*
> *Life is the form,*
> *Where the form is not, there lies the meaning of life."*
> TAO TE KING

The Wheel of Reincarnation: What is Important?

The verse from the "bible" of Taoism also points towards the secret that lies within the immaterial point at the center. Here, where our perception and—more importantly—our intellect end, lies what is essential to the ancient cultures.

All major religions aim for the same center in the mandala. Therefore, conflict between them can never really be about what is essential, but only about issues that are removed from the center. For that reason, this conflict is of little interest to people who regard "religio" as a means of reconnecting with the basis of everything. Take, for example, Christian communion. Whether the wine is actually the blood of Christ (as the Catholics believe) or whether it only symbolizes the blood of Christ (as believed by Protestants) is not the issue. People of both denominations carry the kingdom of God inside them, according to Christ. He never expounded on what he thought communion wine really was, and maybe it wasn't really important to Him. However, He never left us in any doubt that the solution was always to be found within our own hearts, in the center of the most important mandala, the heart chakra. And this links him to other founders of religions, whose followers later sought help in mandalas to express the secret of the center.

In Buddhism, interest is focused on the wheel of reincarnation. Again, everything revolves around the void at the center: it is the declared goal of all Buddhists. In contrast to many western followers of the teachings of reincarnation, their main aim is to leave the spinning wheel of polar life as quickly as possible, in order to find deliverance in the transcendence of the center. They believe that everything and nothing is in the void of the center. In this center, a person who is searching can experience that oneness. All beginnings are found at the center; the end of all things is also there.

"You shall not make for yourself any idol."

Muslims were practically the only ones who adhered to the second Christian commandment not to make any idols or images. They had no other choice than to embrace the mandala because it never attempts to show any image of god whatsoever. God, or unity, is not really represented in the mandala, but we can sense they are present in the center. Whatever point we assert to be the center, that's definitely where it is not. All we can do is picture it as an idea within the mandala.

Embracing the world of ornamental designs was not a guarantee of remaining true to the original teachings, as the history of Islam has shown. The month of fasting, Ramadan, has been reduced to a farce—just like Lent in Christianity—and (un)holy wars are fought everywhere. Actually, they could learn from their own mystics, the Sufis and dervishes, who believe that war is only inner war with one's ego.

Islamic Mandala

Hindu Mandala Blossoms

In Hinduism, most mandalas are based on familiar symbolism or on symbolism that can be easily decoded thanks to our knowledge of the ancient principles. The four great gates located at the four points of the compass say that if we are coming from the material world (represented by the number four), we can gain access to the secret of the center from all directions. The inside is dominated by round structures which point to unity. In Hinduism, the petals of the lotus play a very important part. The lotus flower is the one symbol of development—we often see Buddha sitting on an open lotus flower. The closed lotus bud, which grows upwards through the mud of the pond and finally emerges, represents—with its mandala shape—the lowest chakra, while the open and bright white flower represents the open crown chakra. This flawless mandala star will never again come into contact with the swamp below, but it had to grow from it. By understanding such deep symbolism, Hindus save themselves a lot of sorrow when dealing with darkness and light. For this reason, lotus petals play an important part in the representation of the chakras.

In the east, many temples are built in a mandala shape. The temples of the outside world help to find the center of one's inner temple. At the center of Indian mandalas, we can find some symbols unique to that culture, and some others more familiar to us from other cultures, such as the hexagram from Judaism.

Shri-Mandala

The Hexagram as a Symbol that Links Cultures

Many cultures know the meaning of this symbol in connection with Above and Below, such as the seal of Solomon, the Star of David, and just the hexagram. The triangles of heaven and earth intertwine and make it clear how the two realms are related and interdependent.

With the Star of David, we also remember the hexagram as a terrible witness of recent history. Such symbols as such are really neither good nor bad, but they can be used and abused in all sorts of ways. The use of the Star of David was introduced by Swiss civil servants because they wanted to be able to recognize more quickly all the Jews who were fleeing from the Third Reich. The Nazis then abused it for the worst discrimination imaginable, but the Danish king made it a symbol of honor and human greatness in the same context. When Nazi troops occupied Denmark and forced the Jews to wear the yellow Star of David, the Danish king appeared with the same star on his lapel when he faced his people for a speech the next day.

An Antique Dance Around the Center

This mandala from antiquity reveals the deep understanding of its symbolism at that time. Shape and content go together in a special way. Even though the dance around the center inside every single atom (the concept of the atom had just been mentioned by Democritus) and the spiral patterns within our genes and those of our galaxy had not yet been discovered, the people of antiquity nevertheless knew about the deeper meaning of the mandala. Their circular dances are simply a physical expression of this knowledge.

Until fairly recent times, circular dances were performed in Christian churches, and there are labyrinths to bear witness to this. The most famous of them was discovered in Chartres. You will find more information about Christian labyrinths in my book *Mandalas of the World*.

The ceramic painting opposite shows a lively dance around the center that is a mandala in both shape and design. Only rarely can we see the element of movement, which is essential to all mandalas, represented so beautifully. This motif was found at the bottom of a terracotta beaker and shows Herakles fighting with Triton, the son of the sea god Poseidon. Dancing around the outside are the Nereids, mysterious sea nymphs from the realm of Poseidon (Neptune).

The Romans

A mandala also tells us about the Romans. The cultures on which our society is based were themselves based on mandalas. The Romans adopted many things from the Greek culture, but they were already very familiar with the mandala. For instance in their culture of war, the round shield was indispensable. Senior legionnaires, such as officers, would carry shields that were very ornate mandalas. The shield was the warrior's own mandala, carrying the coat of arms of his family or house, as protection in the figurative sense.

The Coliseum in Rome

A Theater and a Mandala

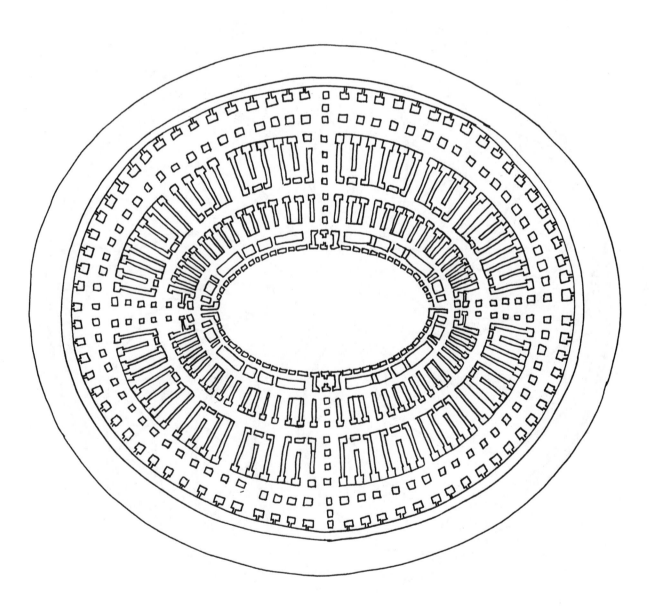

Germanic Mandalas

The Germanic tribes were certainly up to something different than the Romans, but they also built upon the mandala. We can find it in the early warrior societies, such as the Scythians, Goths, Saxons, etc., who were not really interested in art or the ancient principle of Venus. Below is an example from their culture showing a sun wheel from Gotland, Sweden.

Saxon Mandala

This mandala shows how well the Celtic tradition survived the Saxon conquest. In the brooch shown below, the Saxons combined their own motifs with already existing Celtic patterns.

Celtic Mandala

This mandala shows the typical Celtic knot at the center.

Greek Mandala

This mandala shows the sun god Apollo in a floor mosaic.

Italian-Christian Mandala

Jewish Mandala

Egyptian Mandala

Sumerian Seal

This is from about 4,000 B.C.E.

Indian Mandala

This shows the god Krishna dancing with the Gopis, the shepherd girls. The chain of male and female dancers symbolizes the unity of heaven and earth. This motif was found on a wedding shawl and is a representation of the Indian version of the unio mystica.

Chinese Mandala

This mandala depicts a dragon, which is regarded as a symbol of good fortune in China. The Chinese emperors carried it as their emblem. In principle, it is the same dragon that was slain by Herakles, Siegfried, and many other heroes of antiquity. It is interesting that this powerful creature with its many heads is recognized as symbol of good fortune in China, quite the opposite from the way the dragon is judged in western cultures.

African Mandala

Australian Aboriginal Mandala

Mandalas in Places of Worship

The beautiful presence of the mandala is most evident in the design of religious buildings. If man is tuned into the mandala from head to toe, then religious buildings are likewise, from the ceiling to the floor, from heaven to earth. Looking up into the cupola of an Islamic mosque, we can see the same ancient principles that are applied in a Buddhist temple or a Christian cathedral, as is shown below.

A View of the Christian Heavenly World of Angels

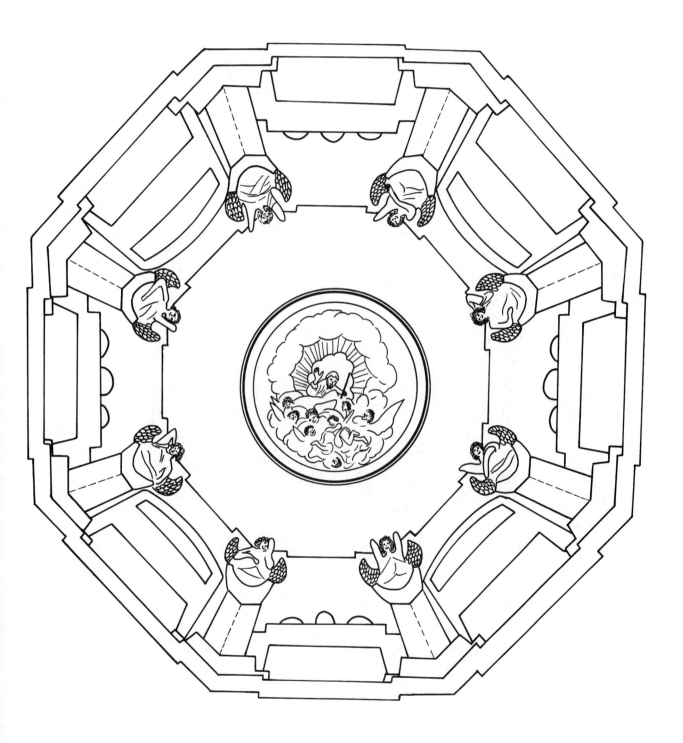

Seven Christian Heavens over Rome

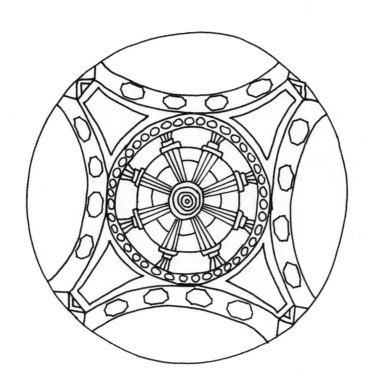

Four Islamic Paradises from the Orient

Cupola Mandala from the Mosque of Sultan Soliman I in Constantinople

Islamic Paradise

184

Two Skies from a Mosque

185

A Sky Mandala over Tibet

A Sky Mandala over Ancient China

According to Confucian beliefs, the ceiling in the Hall of Prayer for Good Harvest in the Temple of Heaven at Beijing shows the geometrical structure of the sky.

Back to the Floor

This now takes us to other mandalas, such as these floor mosaics in the cathedral of Sienna in Italy.

Cathedral Floor Mosaic in Siena

The Wheel of Fortune

The subject of the tenth tarot card in the Catholic cathedral of Sienna might be able to show us how close the link between Christianity and the spiritual tradition once was. The stonemason's lodges that created the cathedrals and eventually brought forth the Freemasons did not see any conflicts in their time. If we remind ourselves that Catholic universities never thought twice about teaching astrology (or what we would refer to as ancient principles today), we might get an even better idea of this closeness.

Floor Mosaic in Siena, Italy

Floor Mosaic in Siena, Italy

190

Floor Mosaic in Siena, Italy

191

Christianity is based on Judaism in the same way as the New Testament is based on the Old Testament. Both churches and synagogues are frequently built on mandala-shaped patterns and outlines. Below, you can see the floor mosaic of a synagogue in Galilee.

The Outline of a Christian Church Tower in Seville, Spain

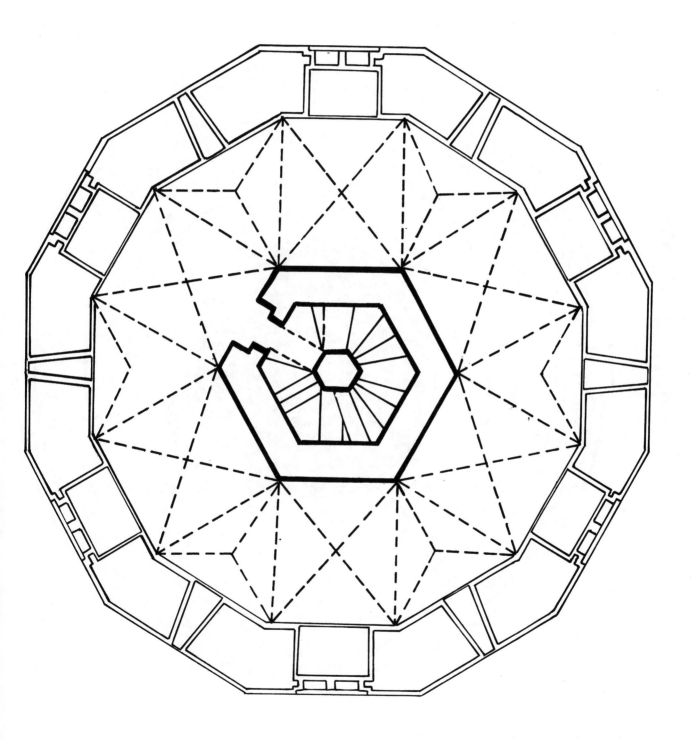

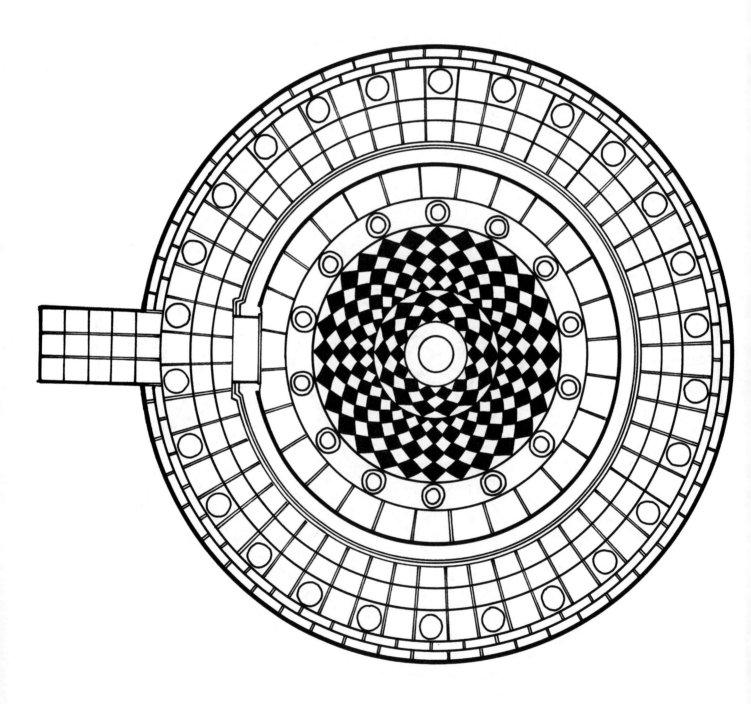

Thelos Temple of Aesculapius in Epidaurus, Greece

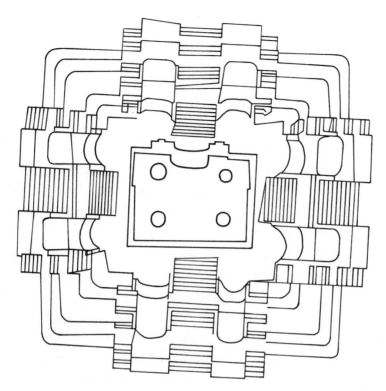

Pyramid of the Mayan Uaxactun

Outline of the Golden City by C.G. Jung

The Primeval Vortex of Creation in Different Cultures and Times

Early humans cannot really have known about the Big Bang or about the spiral shape of our galaxy, the Milky Way. They were missing another dimension because they thought the earth was a disc-mandala and not a sphere-mandala. In other concepts as well, they had to discover the third dimension, such as in art. But they did know about the primeval vortex, which created everything. Perhaps it was through remembering or reliving the experiences of conception and death, in which the vortex plays a very important part.

In a dzong, a monastic fortress in Bhutan, there is a mandala that is thousands of years old which shows a wonderful representation of the universe and its revolving celestial bodies (see the mandala on page 155), but its origin cannot be explained. It was created at a time when culture was still a thing of the future and science did not even exist. However, the many spirals found in Neolithic cultures, including those of the Celtic and Germanic peoples, show a deep understanding of the laws of creation.

Wherever we look, we always find, to this day, representations of vortices at the heart of the matter, from the double helixes of our DNA to physicists' bubble chambers, where they witness the formation of new matter.

Greek Mandala

This is from a shard of pottery dating back to around 3,000–2,000 B.C. The spiral shape in its many variations is particularly evident in this example. In this case, the spiral is meant to represent a perfect human being.

Different Versions of the Primeval Vortex

The Indians represented the primeval vortex, from which they believed everything else developed, in the shape of the three Gunas: the three primeval forces. The unity, which extends via polarity to trinity, is a subject that interested many cultures. The Celts expressed the primeval vortex in a very similar way in this ancient mandala.

To this day, Native Americans design the spiral mandala in a way very similar to that of the Assyrians thousands of years ago.

Germanic Primeval Vortex

The Germanic tribes also seem to have known about the moving basic and primeval forces of the beginning, as evidenced in this Germanic spiral mandala.

Modern-Day Mandalas

Even modern-day chaos theory shows the same spiral dynamics in many of its impressive representations.

Mandala Mania

Once the inner eye has been focused on mandalas, they will suddenly appear everywhere. And what might seem like an obsession is actually the wonderful beginning of the realization that in this creation everything is linked to everything else. In all religions and cultures and among people of all races and colors, we come across the mandala. After this cultural excursion, we should be able to value its ancient principle characteristics even better. The ancient principle characteristics are ubiquitous; we can wander off in all directions and encounter them time and time again. The ancient principle does not exist just in the past, but also in the future. Ancient principles exist independent of space and time; they belong, so to speak, to the primeval material from which creation has been fashioned.

An Exercise

The mandala opposite, appropriately colored, can bring us in touch with this primeval material because it really pulls us into the depths of its center. It has its origins in chaos theory and is therefore a child of mathematics. Put up the colored mandala about two yards away from you, direct a strong light onto it, and then gently gaze down to its center. Listen to some appropriate meditation music. You will soon feel that the mandala is alive and can hold you under its spell. Allow about fifteen minutes for this excursion to the center of being.

Computer Creations: the Most Modern Mandalas of All

Our technical world, with all its achievements, is ultimately based on the mandala. For many centuries, our progress has relied mainly on the wheel and its many variations. This has even influenced our emotional realms; and, as a result, many people feel they are only a tiny wheel that is part of a giant mechanism of many more wheels.

With the advent of the computer, we have left the wheels behind for the first time. In contrast to other technological products, it does not contain a mechanism of wheels. Instead, it relies on the polar world of opposites. A computer only distinguishes between plus and minus, and at amazing speeds. We can use the computer to create some beautiful mandalas, as you will see on the following pages.

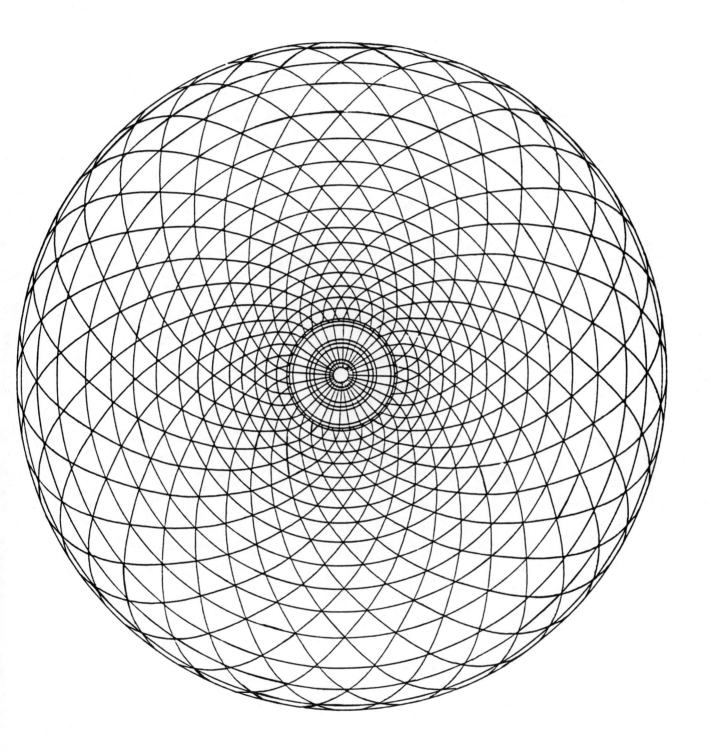

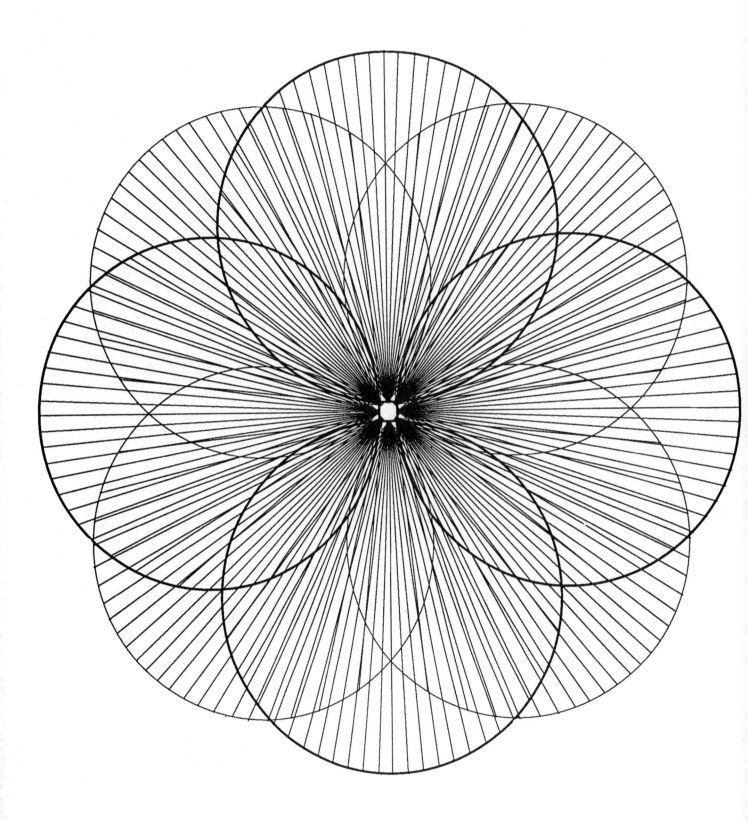

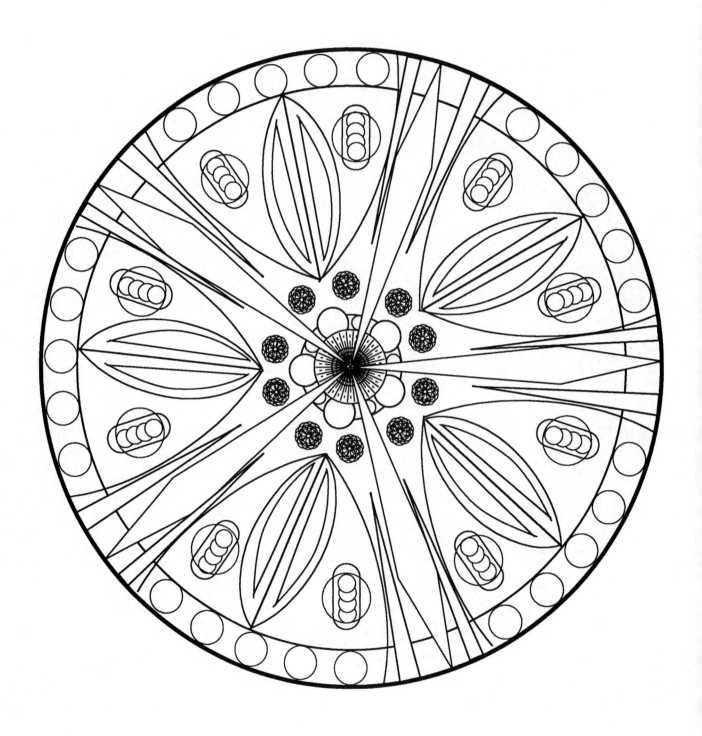

Imitating Old Patterns: the Eternal Expressed in New Ways

With the help of the computer, we can imitate old mandala patterns in amazing ways, just as the most beautiful Gregorian chants can nowadays be "sampled" electronically. We are reminded of window rosettes and cathedrals by mandalas which have all been designed from the keyboard of a skilled computer user.

The Shadow Side of Mandalas

Just like everything else in our creation, mandalas have a shadow side as well. But since they are a perfect representation of creation, the shadows have already been integrated. If we go by the invisible midpoint, which stands for unity, the entire environment—everything that we see as a mandala—is shadow.

There are, however, a few mandala shapes that we might regard as shadows. Every pimple in puberty has the shape of a small volcano and is therefore a mandala. In the case of an abscess, the signature remains the same, only the dimensions are greater. It is like the reaction to a mosquito bite or a bee sting: a mandala. The typical crater of a stomach ulcer is a mandala as well, and so are the gout tophi, the places where the uric acid crystals (themselves mandalas) carry out their painful work.

There are also mandala symptoms such as rotatory vertigo, which is a terrible caricature of spinning dance movements. Furthermore, when we are working with mandalas, it is always a holistic therapy and therefore may bring forth some of the darker sides of our souls. This is really a good sign as far as any therapy is concerned that aims at wholeness, but it will be experienced as something unpleasant. Wholeness and perfection always include everything, which is sometimes forgotten in spiritual circles. The wonderful thing about the mandala is its ability to reconcile all differences in its perfect shape.

Light and Shadow Mandala

A mandala based on an idea by Escher shows clearly that there is a shadow side to everything. As hard as we try to draw only bright white angels, the dark devils appear automatically in their shadows. This is one of the greatest and most difficult subjects in esoteric philosophy, and the main problem of all societies—whether they like to admit it or not.

Mandala Games for Big and Small Children

Mexican legend knows that the gods, if they have nothing else to do, like to play ball, which gives them a connection with the people on earth. On this planet, which itself is a big ball flying through space, pretty much everybody enjoys chasing a ball of some description, from soccer balls and basketballs to tennis and golf balls. Big people are only different insofar as they bring an unnecessary degree of seriousness to the game. Also, over time, they develop the unhealthy tendency to let others play for money and to reduce their own activity to watching. At any rate, everybody likes ball games, and therefore mandalas.

The original meaning behind many games only becomes clear once we are aware of the mandala shape of the ball. The ball is a totem, a symbol of unity, which needs to be taken to a special place along a ritual path. Whether it is soccer or tennis, rugby or volleyball, the ball mandala needs be transported to a certain place, following certain rules, in a ritual which the high priests in their ceremonial garb—also known as referees or umpires—supervise closely. In golf, for example, the goal is to transport a mandala (the ball) onto another mandala (the green), by hitting it in as round a stroke (also a mandala) as possible, and finally putt it into a further mandala (the hole).

If we bear all this in mind, we may be able to imagine how perfectly sensible people, without the slightest chance of ever becoming a golf professional, still experience all the highs and lows of this world when they play this game. Some even start to neglect the really important things in life, such as their families or their jobs, because the small round ball, their mandala totem, does not immediately go where it is supposed to go, namely into the mandala.

Mandala ball games aside, there are plenty of other opportunities to play mandala games, and these have the advantage that the whole family will enjoy them—because according to their mandala character, they appeal to all generations equally.

Below is a fantasy mandala, which you can color in a particularly playful way. You can, for instance, choose the colors without looking and then color with your left hand, assuming you are really right-handed. This mandala is based on a silk painting.

Mandala Puzzle

A mandala game that practices patience like no other involves reassembling a broken jug or other piece of clay pottery. The object of the puzzle is to restore a once perfect pattern. Similar to the way in which coloring in a mandala design corresponds to following one's path through life, reassembling a broken clay jug can lead one to spiritual unity, and it can be a deeply emotional experience. As with the path towards healing, the task here lies in integrating all parts of oneself—the jug in this case—into a whole. It is best to take the steps between multitude and unity in a playful manner. As the jug approaches perfection again, similar steps are possible within the assembler.

A comparable therapeutic experience with the mandala involves throwing pottery on a rotating pottery wheel. Here, we are forced to dive deep into our own center first; otherwise, the lump of clay would fly off the wheel immediately from our lack of concentration.

Reassembling a three-dimensional mandala pattern by restoring a piece of pottery is a familiar game for archeologists, and we can admire the impressive results at many historic sites.

Shards like these will bring good luck, at least if they have contributed to rediscovering one's own wholeness.

The Broken Jug

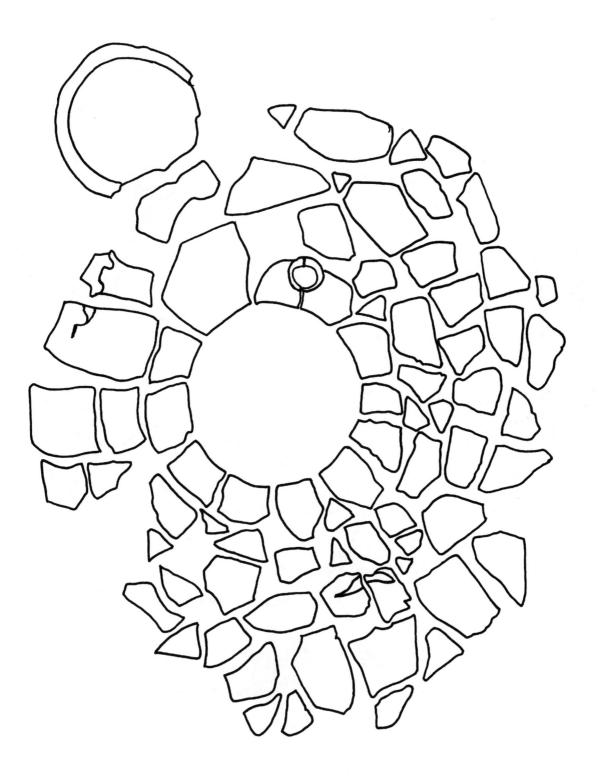

The Healed Jug: From Multitude to Unity

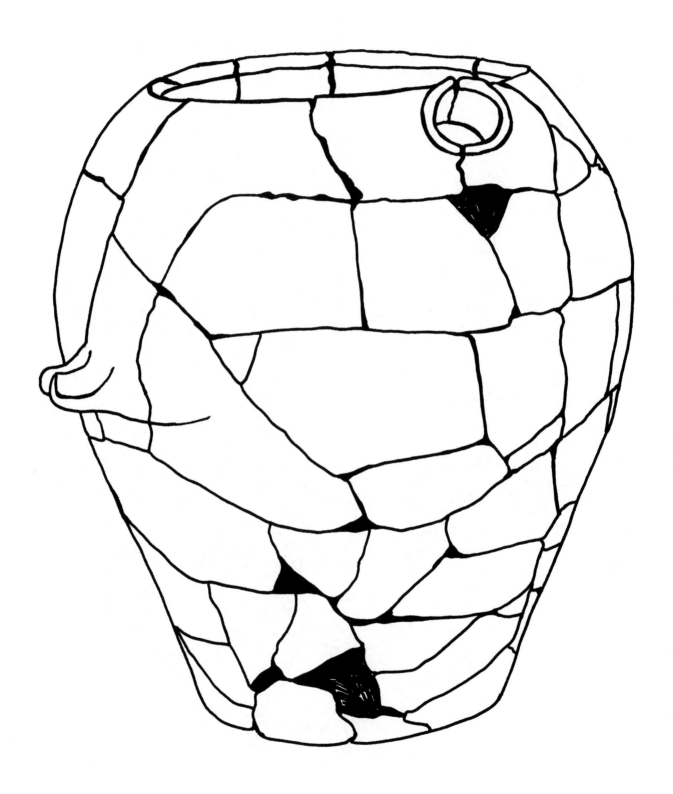

Yin and Yang Mandala Exercise

This half mandala has been shaped by male yang characteristics and desperately needs its other half (or better half, as the saying goes), like the fairy tale hero needs his princess. First, color the existing male half with the appropriate fiery colors and then complete the missing female half with both the corresponding pattern and the appropriate watery colors. The contrast between patterns and colors should be as stark as possible.

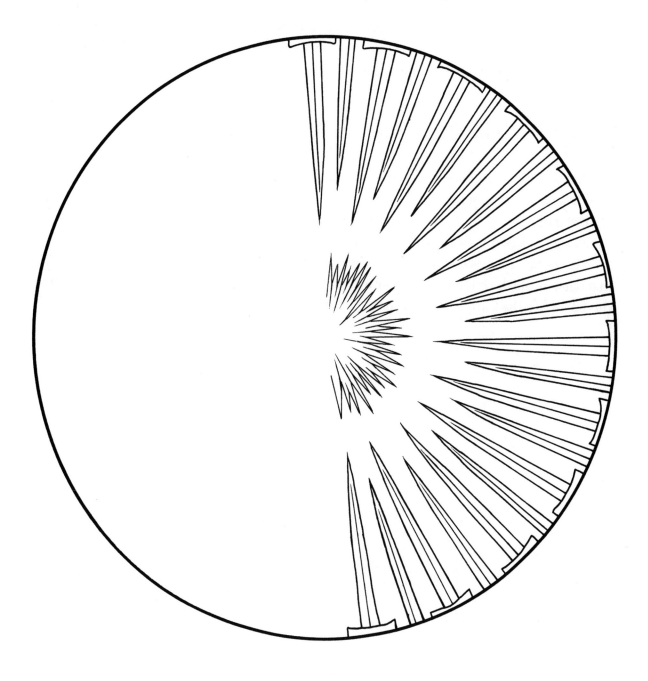

The Family Mandala Calendar

Here, we want to try and capture the right mood for each month in a calendar. It seems logical that the youngest children and the next older siblings should color the mandalas for the spring months, April, May, and June. The older adolescents and young adults should take their turn with the summer months of July and August, although August and especially September should be reserved for the parents, who are approaching the midpoint in life. The months of October, November, and December should be colored by the grandparents, who are perhaps about to retire or who are already pensioners, and January, February, and March by the oldest generation to color, the great-grandparents. A one-year old child could definitely try to color the April mandala.

The Four Seasons Mandala Calendar

It takes slightly less effort to decorate a four seasons mandala calendar according to the qualities each season possesses. We should give every season its colors and shapes. Spring, for instance, should be colored with powerful, bold, aggressive strokes in shades of red, which signal departure and new beginnings.

If we take this one step further, the concept can be extended to a four life-seasons mandala, in which childhood and youth are allocated the first quarter, adult life the second, the fall of life the third, and the evening of life the fourth.

The Native American Mandala of the Four Life Seasons

Paper Mandalas

Paper mandalas are very easy to make. You just fold a piece of paper twice so that there are four layers of paper on top of each other. With a sharp pair of scissors, start at the "thick" corner and cut patterns into the paper, which will make a mandala once the paper is unfolded. With a little bit of practice you will be able to create many surprisingly different circular shapes very quickly. If you then paste transparent paper to the back of the design, you will create a window decoration which children will enjoy not only at Christmas, but all year round.

A similar effect can be achieved by coloring the mandalas with crayons and ironing them on the reverse until the colors become transparent.

You can also create a kind of glass painting by attaching the mandala to a suitable window pane, imitating the effect of stained glass church windows.

221

Living Mandalas

You can make lovely mobiles from smaller mandalas. To emphasize the spherical effect of the mandalas, cut two mandalas up to their midpoints and then slot the two mandalas into each other. Fix the shape with a little bit of tape. You can make as many multi-colored mandala balls as you wish to make your mobile even more charming.

If you are very careful, you can combine the ideas from the previous page with the mobile, adding an interesting light effect to the motion effect. This will be particularly effective if you have pasted transparent paper in different colors to the back of the cutout patterns.

The Christmas Mandala Tree

It is very easy to decorate a Christmas tree with a wealth of mandalas. This way, it will do much more justice to the tree's original symbolism than if it were hung with masses of sweets and candy which, in our affluent times, are certainly not symbols of the light that is growing stronger again. If we consider the deep mysticism of light as captured in Gothic window rosettes (see my book *Mandalas of the World*), the mandala is really the most appropriate decoration for the Christmas tree.

Store-bought balls and straw stars aside (themselves pretty mandalas, of course), you can easily make lovely paper balls in the style of the mobile mandalas. Mandala stars—either drawn or folded and cut—can also play their part in the big Christmas mandala. And even the weeks of advent cannot do without the mandala, as the advent wreath clearly shows.

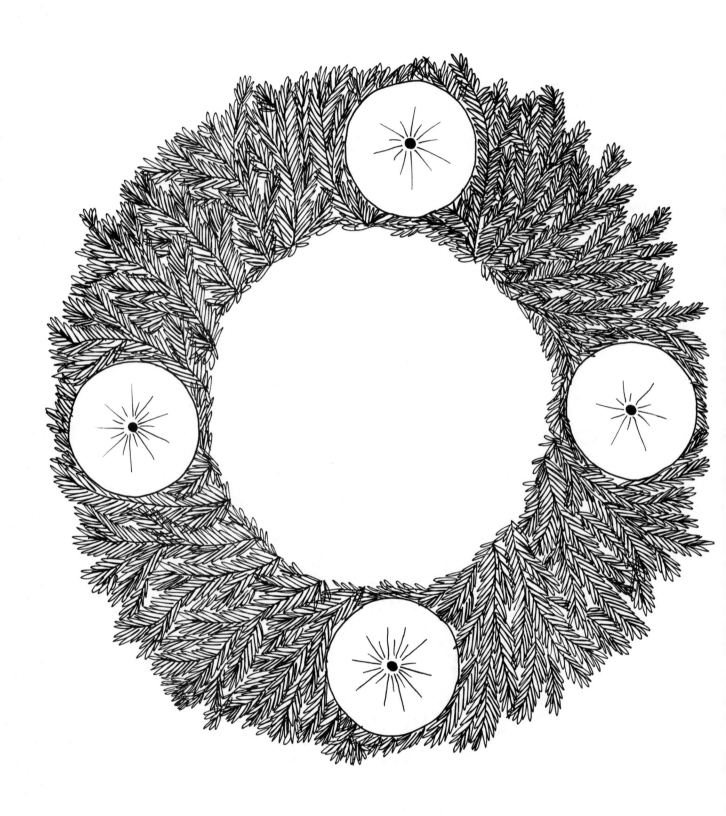

Advent Wreath

Vacation Mandalas

On the beach, you can make beautiful mandalas from shells and other flotsam, which will have the additional attraction that the sea will reclaim them time and time again. This corresponds to the old Tibetan mandala traditions, and also to the Native American ones and most shaman traditions in general, which end the mandala ritual by returning the mandala to nature.

There is no end to the different possibilities of making mandalas from natural materials. It can be very rewarding to make mandalas from fallen leaves, and then leave their destiny to the fall storms, or to make winter mandalas from snow. For instance, if you use appropriately shaped snow wedges, you can make a proper mandala gateway, which will disappear along with winter. It therefore acts as a gauge for the power of winter—once winter loses its grip, the mandala gates will collapse. The first signs of this are visible when the gate seems just a little off balance.

Snow Mandala Arch Based on an Idea by
the Artist Goldsworthy

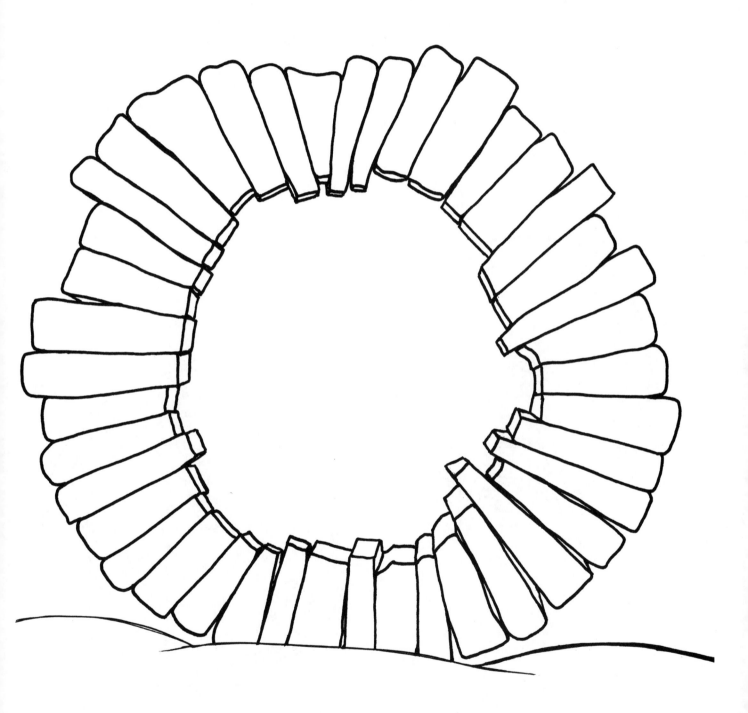

As long as we are able to step through this gate, the power of winter is still strong.

Mandala Games for Young and Old

Apart from the frequently used mandala balls, many other games revolve around the mandala pattern, from a child's spinning top to the hula-hoop of a teenager, from a merry-go-round to a Ferris wheel to the game of roulette, which is for adults only.

The best thing perhaps about these mandala exercises or games is that they are fun, but they also represent a far-reaching kind of therapy—a playful therapy maybe, or a therapeutic game, or maybe just a game. Mandala therapy is always self-therapy and does not require any specialists. We are all mandala specialists, and if any help or advice is required, a mother is much better suited to give it to her child than any mandala scientist at a university.

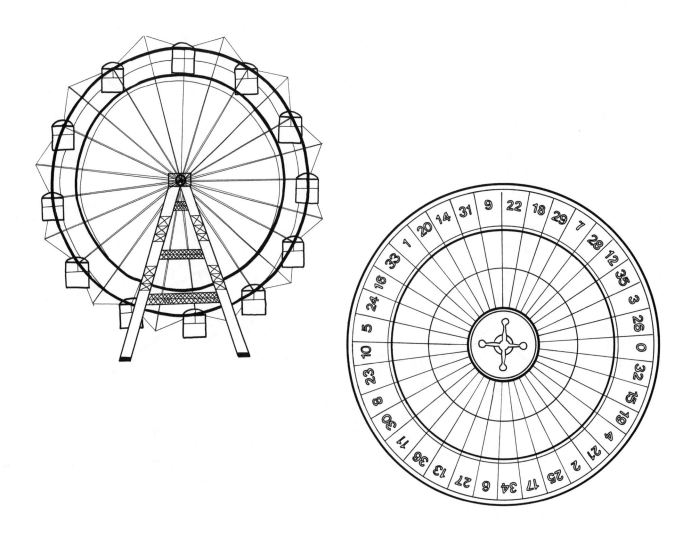

Dancing in the Mandala

All circular or round dances are mandalas, simply because of the shape they draw in a room. All dances require centering; however, we must not lose our own center while dancing, and we must be at rest in our center. Dancing teaches us how to stabilize a fairly unstable center or even how to find one's center in the first place. Dancing through life or experiencing life as a dance are expressions of this knowledge. If you have not found your center, you will not be able to dance through life. This becomes clear not only when looking at the dervishes of Islam, but also at people here who love to waltz. Even modern "free style" dancers need to be aware of their centers, or they will get dizzy and lose their balance.

Garden Mandalas: Esthetically Pleasing Designs

Of course we can install in our gardens mandalas made from cobbles, flagstones, or wooden stakes stuck into the ground. This will create the centering effect mentioned earlier, and the mandala shape alone will be a focal point in the garden. By sitting at the center of such a mandala, you will increase your own concentration.

In the western world, we are slowly getting used to the ideas of Feng Shui and other such philosophies which hold that shapes have an influence on the space that surrounds them. Take the mandala as an example and you can easily experience it yourself.

In this respect, it might be interesting to build a Native American medicine wheel in one's garden, which is very easily done. It would require a little bit of research into Native American symbolism regarding the points of the compass. You would then need to position the mandala with a compass (itself, of course, a mandala) and finally sit and meditate or simply reflect, facing the different points of the compass.

Garden Mandalas for Good Health

You can make an interesting mandala from pebbles of different sizes and colors by pressing them into fresh concrete. This mandala will also have a medical aspect once the concrete has set. If you walk over it with your bare feet, the reflex zones of your feet will be massaged by the pebbles, providing therapy for your whole body.

Living Season Mandalas

You can create a mandala for the spring or even the whole year by planting seeds and bulbs according to a mandala pattern. The whole year through, seasonal plants will then tell you, like a living seasonal clock, how far the year has progressed. Children in particular enjoy the changes that take place in a growing mandala. This idea is based on the herb and flower gardens which traditionally existed in front of old farmhouses.

The summer mandala can be combined with a mandala sundial by planting sunflowers in the shape of a mandala. As sunflowers always turn their heads towards the sun, you will always know what time it is. Experiences like these, with a natural sundial, seem to be much more important for children today than we would like to admit. It is true we have clocks and watches today that are much more exact, but despite developments in measuring time with chronometers that have been calibrated to within a thousandth of a second, it is still much easier for the soul to comprehend with the help of natural experiences. Otherwise, we will look at the picture of a person who knows how to work all the technical gadgets, but does not understand the theory or the workings behind them.

The fall mandala, as described before, should be laid from fallen fruit or leaves. The basic structures can be laid down with the help of leaves that have been fixed to the ground with small sticks.

Winter is best described by the previously mentioned snow gate mandala. It is a wonderful mandala path through the entire year, not just for children.

You can also plant a circle of trees for the whole year, which will always tell you what time of year it is.

And if you have enough space, you can plant a mandala house made of willow. Because of its great vitality and flexibility, you can weave a kind of living igloo from willow, which will—like any mandala—greatly appeal to the children.

The Four Seasons Tree

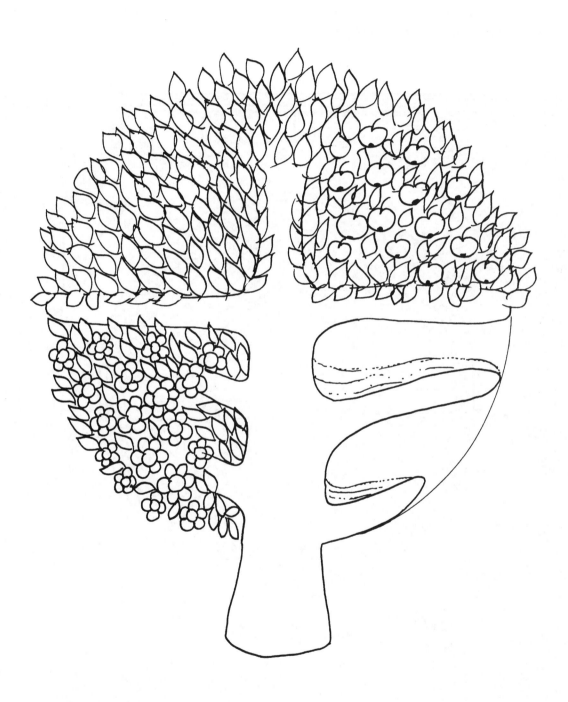

The Wheel of Fortune and the Four Seasons

This representation of a French miniature from the 14th century shows angels turning the wheel of fortune and singing God's praises.

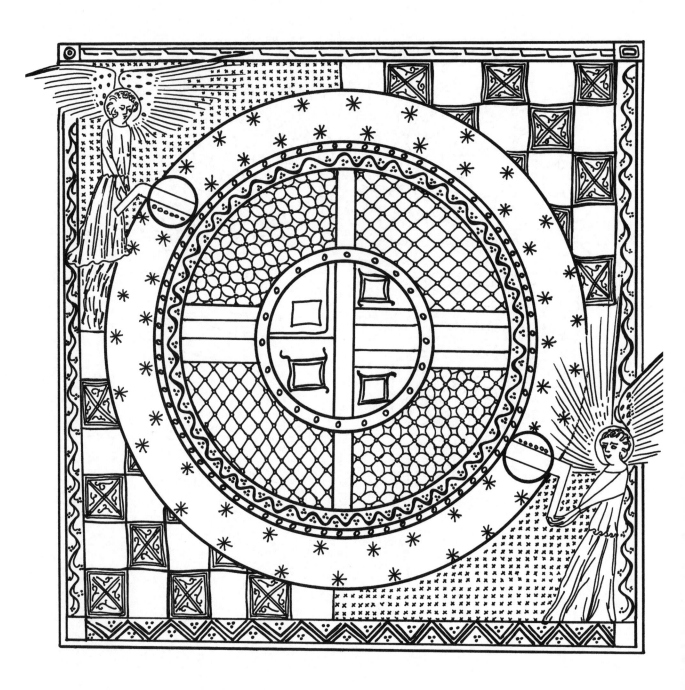

Kitchen Mandalas

The prototype of a kitchen mandala is an apple whose skin has been peeled off in one piece, forming a perfect mandala spiral. Of course, the apple is a mandala before and after peeling, and you could further utilize the apple peel by making an infusion from it.

If the apple is cut into wedges, they too will become a mandala if we let the original apple shape just fall open. If only one wedge is cut from the apple, it will also reveal mandalas in the shape of its core, and then each pip itself is a mandala.

Most types of fruit and vegetable remain mandalas once they have been cut open, or only take on a mandala shape once they have been cut, such as celery or carrots. Others, such as broccoli, are mandalas that are obviously made up of smaller mandalas.

If they are made into meals, the mandala remains the most suitable shape, whether we are talking about salads or baked goods, cold platters or gratins. With a little bit of awareness, we can lift the mandala culture in the kitchen to new heights.

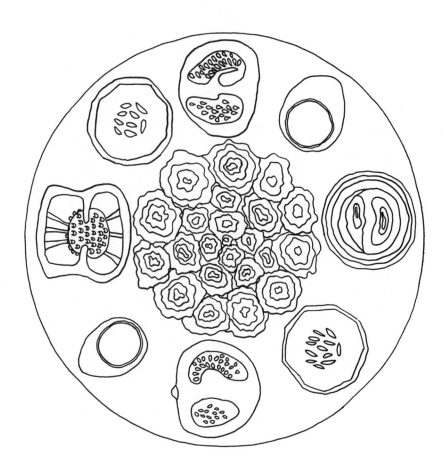

Mandala Arts and Crafts

For many people, art starts with arts and crafts, and there are unlimited possibilities here, as with the mandala in general. Mandalas can be fashioned from almost any material, from carved plates to wrought iron archways.

It may be a wonderful experience if you have the opportunity to blow a glass mandala, and you may find a class somewhere that teaches this art.

Basket weaving also creates mandalas most of the time.

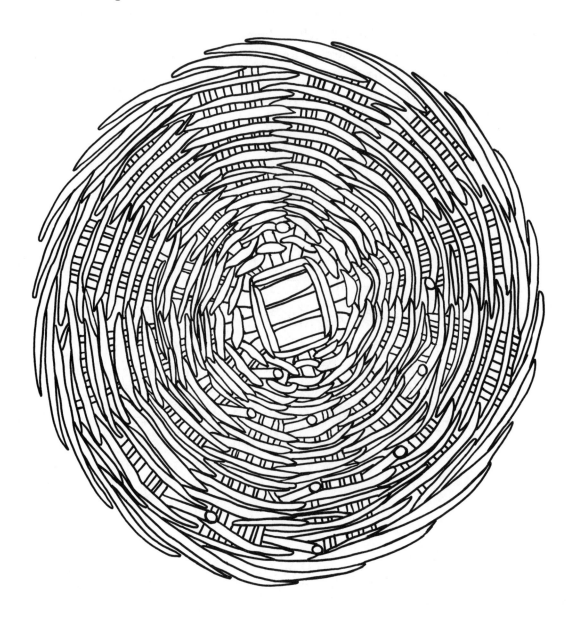

Art Inside the Mandala

Leaving crafts behind, the path to mandala-shaped art has been preordained, and we have already encountered it in the impressive nature mandalas by Goldsworthy. One of the highlights of mandala art are the painted and jewel-encrusted mandalas by Marlies Laduree. They provide a link to the medieval church window mandalas, which were also pieces of art of inestimable value.

A Mandala Based on an Idea by Marlies Laduree.

A Final Mandala

These footprints in the sand, which will be washed away by the next wave, close the circle of mandalas, which—of course—can be opened again with every individual mandala. The path leads from the center to the center, or as the Indians say, "From here to here."

Mandala: All of us who have drawn the mandalas, Elisabeth Mitteregger, Julia and Andrea Druckenthaner and Willi Weis, my wife Margit, my daughter Naomi and I, as the author, would like to thank you for following us this far, right into the center of the mandala. We hope that you will go much further, until you reach your own center.

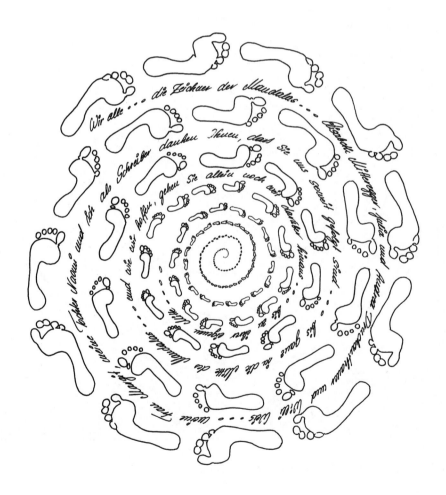

INDEX